"*Made Like Martha* will infuse your life with a fresh perspective as you learn to embrace your God-given personality and also discover how—and when—to rest and retreat."

—KAREN EHMAN, Proverbs 31 Ministries speaker and author of *Keep It Shut*

"For those who long to get off the merry-go-round of striving, Katie's words are a welcome invitation to let go of trying harder and instead rest in your identity as a beloved daughter."

—HOLLEY GERTH, author of *You're Already Amazing*

"*Made Like Martha* is my new go-to gift for leaders, hard workers, and passionate women who long to listen to God's voice and know ⌐   when they're tempted to hustle."

—BEKAH JANE POGUE, author of *Choosing Real*

"Katie Reid reveals how much God loves doer   and their identity in Him while they live out their c⌐

—CAROL KENT, speaker and auth⌐

"Katie will take you and your weary Mar   journey to abundant freedom. If you are a doer, do yourself a favor   ead this book. And all the Marthas sing 'hallelujah!'"

—JAMI AMERINE, author of *Stolen Jesus*

"I was a doer until I was diagnosed with a serious illness. In *Made Like Martha*, Katie Reid helped me recalibrate and find strength in service and peace, even when busy and weak."

—JAN GREENWOOD, Equip pastor at Gateway Church and author of *Women at War*

"*Made Like Martha* is the gospel for go-getters. Within these pages, Reid silences the voices that push, 'Do more. Be more. Achieve more.' Those persistent taunts are covered by the glorious blanket of God's lavish grace and unconditional love."

—KATE MOTAUNG, author of *A Place to Land*

"This book was just what my Martha-heart needed. I felt affirmed in who I am and learned how to find peace and rest in the midst of my busy life."

—JENNIFER DUKES LEE, author of *The Happiness Dare* and *Love Idol*

"In a world that often praises Mary for pausing to spend time with the Lord, Katie shares the Father's heart for the women He made to be like Martha. It will bring freedom and rest to all who read it."
—BECKY THOMPSON, author of *Love Unending* and *Hope Unfolding*

"If you identify more as Martha than Mary, you will rejoice in learning how to stay calm in the chaos, how to find a balance between striving and slowing down, and how to finally rejoice in the woman God created you to be."
—KATE BATTISTELLI, author of *Growing Great Kids*

"Reading *Made Like Martha* was the first time I felt as though someone acknowledged the overachiever parts of my personality as something good and then reminded me that I'm also called beloved."
—MARY CARVER, blogger and coauthor of *Choose Joy*

"*Made Like Martha* takes you on a gentle, truth-filled journey to the freedom you perhaps don't even realize your soul is craving."
—VANESSA HUNT, coauthor of *Life in Season* and founder of AtThePicketFence.com

"Katie combines poignant storytelling and powerful Scripture teaching into an invitation for us to lay aside our personal expectations and to-do lists and embrace the call of Christ—not to do, but to be."
—TERI LYNNE UNDERWOOD, author of *Praying for Girls*

"Doers can finally breathe a sigh of relief and find rest in who God created them to be. Katie's words bring freedom to stop striving and start thriving as His beloved daughter."
—ERIN H. WARREN, women's ministry director at First Baptist Orlando

"What a beautiful invitation to leave the try-hard life behind and just belong to Jesus! This Martha is grateful."
—JOANNA WEAVER, author of *Having a Mary Heart in a Martha World*

"When you're exhausted from the try-hard, dizzy-busy life of striving to accomplish it all, while attempting to do it better than before, this message of hope, truth, and freedom is the rest you need."
—JEN SCHMIDT, author of *Just Open the Door*

"For the overwhelmed woman attempting to do it all, this is an invitation to freedom."
—WENDY SPEAKE, coauthor of *Triggers, Parenting Scripts,* and *Life Creative*

KATIE M. REID

Made Like Martha

Good News
for the Woman Who
Gets Things Done

FOREWORD BY LISA-JO BAKER

WATERBROOK

MADE LIKE MARTHA

Trade Paperback ISBN 978-0-7352-9126-3
eBook ISBN 978-0-7352-9132-4

Cover design by Kelly L. Howard

Published in the United States by WaterBrook, an imprint of the Crown Publishing Group, a division of Penguin Random House LLC, New York.

WATERBROOK® and its deer colophon are registered trademarks of Penguin Random House LLC.

Library of Congress Cataloging-in-Publication Data
Names: Reid, Katie, author.
Title: Made like Martha : good news for the woman who gets things done / Katie M. Reid.
Description: First Edition. | Colorado Springs : WaterBrook, 2018. | Includes bibliographical references.
Identifiers: LCCN 2017045448| ISBN 9780735291263 (pbk.) | ISBN 9780735291324 (electronic)
Subjects: LCSH: Martha, Saint. | Christian women--Religious life.
Classification: LCC BS2480.M3 R45 2018 | DDC 248.8/43–dc23
LC record available at https://lccn.loc.gov/2017045448

Printed in the United States of America
2018—First Edition

10 9 8 7 6 5 4 3 2 1

SPECIAL SALES
Most WaterBrook books are available at special quantity discounts when purchased in bulk by corporations, organizations, and special-interest groups. Custom imprinting or excerpting can also be done to fit special needs. For information, please email specialmarketscms@penguinrandomhouse.com or call 1-800-603-7051.

To Adam.
Thank you for loving this modern Martha, even when it's hard work. Thank you for teaching me about grace—without using many words. Thank you for sitting with me in a hammock on Wednesday nights at 9:00 p.m.; it is one of the best things we do.

To Brooklyn, Kaleos, Banner, Isaiah, and Larkin.
You are five of my favorite chapters in the story God is writing. I love you more than words.

As they were traveling along, He entered a village; and a woman named Martha welcomed Him into her home. She had a sister called Mary, who was seated at the Lord's feet, listening to His word. But Martha was distracted with all her preparations; and she came up to Him and said, "Lord, do You not care that my sister has left me to do all the serving alone? Then tell her to help me." But the Lord answered and said to her, "Martha, Martha, you are worried and bothered about so many things; but only one thing is necessary, for Mary has chosen the good part, which shall not be taken away from her."

—LUKE 10:38–42, NASB

Contents

PART III: *Standing*

Bible Study for Individuals and/or Groups

Foreword

I grew up in a home where my mom died a week after I turned eighteen and my dad fled his grief in a shotgun remarriage, which ended in a quickie divorce. I felt the bits and pieces of my life dissolving between my fingers and feared that if I didn't grab the reins, no one else would. This is not a wise choice for a college kid. Or a grown-up. Or a grandma. But it would take me a couple more decades to learn that. The hard way.

I believed that if I could will people into living a certain way, making certain choices, talking in certain kinds of tones and voices, then I could make life better for them. But really, what I meant deep down in my bones and DNA is that if I could make them behave a certain way, life would be better for me.

Katie and I have this in common: the need to take charge and take initiative and take all need for faith out of the equation—because we've worked hard enough on behalf of everyone around us, including God. We've got this, and we've got ourselves convinced that if we want things done right, we've got to do them ourselves.

I think it goes without saying that this is exhausting.

My shoulders, like Katie's, have sagged for years under the weight of my self-imposed obligations, as well as the weight of resistance I encountered in my siblings, my kids, and my husband, who weren't interested in having their lives dictated to them. But for the longest time, I didn't know how to let go. I didn't know God well enough to believe that He was capable of holding us all together when I'd lived through us all crashing apart.

Katie describes it like this: "It is a good thing to be reliable, but there is a sneaky shift that can happen from being responsible to putting ourselves in charge of things that aren't ours to manage."

I've spent years consciously trying to stop taking control of the things that aren't mine to manage. And of all the lessons I've learned, the most important is that other people are not ours to manage. They're ours to love. Ours to forgive. Ours to lead and lean on and lean into. They're ours to embrace and accept and challenge and befriend and learn from. *But they are not ours to manage.*

Other people—all of them—belong to the God who designed their blueprints, their souls, and their stories. And as it turns out, I am not the boss of any of that. This was a shocking discovery to me. But the relief! The massive relief of not having to carry the weight of every decision everyone else around me was making. It was so huge that I nearly toppled over once it had fallen off my back.

And reading Katie's words was like rereading my own story of discovering this truth—the truth that maybe should be obvious but certainly wasn't to me. Maybe it's not obvious to you either. Maybe you're holding on with white knuckles to a vision of how you want the people around you to look, act, and decide—and you're about to pass out from the frustration of it all. Listen, let Katie help you loosen your grip on what comes next. This book will walk you through the tender process of first simply letting go of the decisions that aren't yours to make in the first place and then trusting a much more trustworthy Architect to catch it all in His safe hands.

It's probably easier and more difficult than you expect.

But it will be liberating. I am certain.

This isn't about changing your gifts, your drive, or your ability to multitask. This is about unloading the unnecessary—those things that have snuck onto your to-do list that really aren't yours to do. This is about making room for all the ways in which you are wired to excel, without being held back by all the ways in which you feel you fail. Because there's no such thing as perfect people, perfect performances, or perfect endings—not when it comes to ourselves, the people around our tables, in our offices, or branching out from our family trees.

Here's to letting Katie walk us through what that might look like, in real time. I believe she is a trusted guide, and her goal is the same as our Father God's: to set us free, so that we might be released into the fullness of the unique and phenomenal talents He has built into our DNA. Not to change that but rather to see it multiplied way beyond what our limited lists could ever have asked or imagined.

—Lisa-Jo Baker, best-selling author of *Never Unfriended*,
from her dining room table in Hanover, Maryland

Company's Coming!

I am determined to make a good impression. A whirlwind of activity, like a ceiling fan on steroids, precedes the arrival of our honored guest.

I bark orders. "Hurry up! We're running out of time, people!" The to-do list is long and our company will be here soon.

Declutter.

Swish toilets.

Vacuum.

Make sure dinner doesn't burn!

Cut fresh flowers for a centerpiece.

"Who spilled cereal and didn't clean it up? You guys are killing me here!" Hop to it, step it up, get it done. Marching in double time, we feel frustration build as we dash to get the house presentable. "Set the table, and please remember to use the good silverware."

Ding-dong.

I wipe away a bead of sweat as I cross another item off the list.

Deep breath.

Trying to forget the careless words spoken as we scrambled to tidy up, I put on a happy face before I open the poppy-orange door. "Oh, hello there. So honored you could come."

I spy a stray sock and kick it under the shoe rack like a ninja.

"I'm glad you invited me over," he says.

"Of course. Anything for you," I gush.

"May I sit down?"

"Sure! Make yourself at home."

He walks in and looks around.

I cringe as I notice a cobweb overhead that I'm afraid he'll point out. Covertly, I swat it down before following him out of the room. *Big sigh of relief. He didn't seem to notice.* He enters the family room.

"That recliner looks nice," he says.

"Oh, that old thing? Are you sure you want to sit there, Jesus?"

"Absolutely."

He wastes no time making himself comfortable.

"Can I get you something to drink?" I offer.

"Oh, no thank you. I'm good."

"Are you—?"

Buzz! Buzz!

"Oh! That must be the pie. Gotta check it. My sister will keep you company. I have a few more things to get done."

PART I

Striving

You don't have to
strive for what you
already have.

I

The Big To-Do

God's Love for the Doer's Heart

∽

You don't have to earn anyone's love anymore.
Believe this: That you are already God's beloved.

—Jennifer Dukes Lee

I am a Martha fan. A lot has been said, written, and broadcast about dear Martha and her sister, Mary, based on their story in Luke 10. But Martha often gets a bad rap. While I'm not here to rehash what's already been discussed, I do want to address the misconception that there is *something wrong* with being like her. After all, Martha welcomed Jesus into her home. Some versions of the Bible say she "opened her home to him" (verse 38, NIV) or "received him into her house" (KJV).

Welcomed. Opened. Received. These words paint a bright picture of hospitality. Martha was probably a mint-on-the-pillow type of hostess. A take-charge woman who accomplished tasks in a timely manner, she was probably the type of gal who managed a myriad of details. She wasn't idle or lazy and likely spent her days in a flurry of activity. When I read about biblical Martha, I envision her as strong and savvy—a to-do list kind of woman.

Responsible. *Check.*

Capable. *Check.*

Willing. *Check.*

Most of the time I am that way too. And being a woman who handles it all takes its toll. In the mirror I see a modern Martha who finds herself frustrated because she's not wired like biblical Martha's sister. You know, Mary—the sister who chose what was "better" (verse 42, NIV), the "necessary" thing (NASB), the "one thing" (NASB), the "good part" (NASB)? I try to unzip my design as a doer and shed the skin of efficiency because I interpret the passage in Luke to mean that Mary is the poster child for getting it right. Since I spend most of my days bustling instead of sitting at Jesus's feet, I feel as if something is inherently wrong with me. *Mary is right. Martha is wrong. Good Mary. Bad Martha.*

Mary's temperament seems approved. Martha's temperament seems discounted. And because I identify with and live like Martha the doer, I feel wrong—or at least not quite right. I like approval, so you can imagine the tug-of-war that transpires within my soul as I grapple with the Mary ideal versus the Martha reality. But the tension goes further and deeper than that.

Although the lie—that love will be withheld or removed if I don't get "it" right—is buried, I buy into it. (Insert your own "it" here: appearance, job, pants size, housework, marriage, parenting, friendships, and so on.) While getting all these "its" right is important to me, getting faith right is the driving force behind try-hard living. Because daily quiet time, praying without ceasing, and being still are not working out so well, I feel as though my wiring is flawed. I assume that love is limited because I don't measure up.

My friend Brandi shares similar thinking. While recently chaperoning a field trip at a local bounce house, we wasted no time jumping into deep conversation as our kids raced around the inflatable jungle gym. Brandi said that she grew up knowing she needed a Savior, but the idea that God loved her and thought she was special sounded crazy. It seemed to her that His fond affection was reserved for those who were more talented, more beautiful, or more holy. She was convinced God's eye did not fall on her as He scanned the great big earth He created. His loving gaze smiled on the missionaries and the pastors and everyone else "doing it right" but not on her—the one who felt like a hot mess and seemed doomed to repeat mistakes.

Brandi also mentioned that several years ago on a particularly heart-wrenching day, she poured out these thoughts to someone she trusted. Despite this woman's assurance that, yes, God did see her and love her, Brandi still struggled to believe it. As Brandi left her meeting with this woman, she went to a drive-through to buy some chili for lunch. As she waited to pay, she checked her appearance in the mirror. Her blotchy face reflected her broken heart. Her bloodshot eyes reflected her broken spirit. She put on sunglasses to mask her hurt. As she reached out to pay for her meal, the woman at the window stopped her. "The person ahead of you paid for your food. She asked me to give you a message: 'God loves you.'"

These were the words Brandi desperately wanted to believe. God provided the spiritual food she hungered for. Jesus loved *her*. She didn't have to improve herself, go into ministry, or alter her temperament to be adored by the One who made her and saved her. In the middle of a taxing day, in the simplest of ways, God assured Brandi of her position in His heart.

Before her drive-through encounter, Brandi felt she had to be more or be someone else to be deemed worthy of God's affections. And I wonder whether Martha felt the same way.

Did Martha try to prove her worth through exemplary behavior? *Look at what I can do! See all I can manage? My shoulders ache, my tone is edgy, but by golly, I get things done.*

That's how I feel sometimes—actually, *many* times. My tense posture is a response to external and internal expectations to do more, be more, and look good doing it. Inferiority and superiority duke it out in an ugly feud that leaves me weary and bruised.

Frustrated. *Check.*

Stressed. *Check.*

Overwhelmed. *Check.*

Striving, driving, and producing become the fuel to earn love and stay in good standing with the Savior. My good works become a means to obtaining favor, and I'm afraid they're not good enough. And neither am I. It feels as though my approval is based on how well I perform, and I fear rejection if that performance is subpar.

I cringe at the thought of one of my less-than-stellar days being documented for all to read, analyze, and criticize as Martha's has been throughout the years.

Jesus corrects Martha because she is worried and bothered about many things. When I read the account of Jesus coming to Mary and Martha's home in Luke 10, I usually hear verses 41 and 42 as a scolding from the Lord: "Martha, Martha, you are anxious and troubled about many things, but one thing is necessary. Mary has chosen the good portion, which will not be taken away from her." I read between the lines, *"You're not enough. You need to improve to be accepted. You need to try harder to be loved. Do better, be better, Martha."*

As I said in a guest post on a blog,

I am hard on myself. I constantly critique, over-analyze, and expect more of myself than is humanly possible. I work hard to stay on top of things . . . so that I . . . stay above disapproving gazes.

I strive to be the best woman, the best wife, the best mom, the best friend, and I miss the mark again and again.

Since I walk on a high tightrope of unreasonable expectations, I am positioned to topple at the smallest criticism.

The kids disobey. I slip.
The laundry isn't put away—ever. I trip.
The book proposal is rejected. I limp.
I fall from the heights and land hard.[1]

My worth gets tangled up in my works, so I walk with a spiritual limp. And because I hold myself to the Mary Poppins standard of being "practically perfect in every way," I am often discouraged. I'm worn out from trying to be everything to everyone and fed up with messing up. Capable is my middle name, yet if I'm honest, I'm a few yeses away from falling apart.

The bustle causes shallow breathing. The hustle produces a preoccupation with self. The scurry gives birth to stress. The hurry makes my body ache. Words lash out. All this pushing tires my soul. The proving steals peace. The multitasking overwhelms. The merry-go-round of striving leaves my head spinning and stomach churning. The kids need me, the husband wants me, work is waiting, dinner needs a plan, the bills need paying, the house needs dusting—wait, I don't dust or iron (please, no judging). Something's gotta give! I want to be enough, yet I've had enough of this dizzying ride. There must be another way, a better way, off this Ferris wheel of fret.

I can't bear another lecture or scolding.

I'm tired. And the sleep isn't as sweet when I try to carry the world on my shoulders, which ache as my thoughts swirl overhead like a tornado.

HIS SIDE

When our kids have bad dreams, they race down the hallway, feet pattering from wood floor to blue shag, as they seek comfort at our bedside. Although I sleep closer to the door, they usually go to my husband's side of the bed. Sleep deprivation is not my friend, and if I am woken up at night, Mean Lady emerges. I have an edge and impatience to my voice. I don't intend to be this way, but a sharp-tongued beast surfaces when provoked.

The other day I told Adam, "The kids need to stop coming in and waking us up! We need to get a full night's sleep."

I anticipated he'd agree, but he said, "We're their parents, and it's our job to comfort them when they need it." Even if it's the middle of the night. Even if it's inconvenient.

Conviction.

Then it came flooding back—the time our son Banner came to my side and I pretended to be asleep so he'd go to Adam's side instead. He was about five years old at the time. In the dark I saw his round face staring at me, seeing whether I was awake. I closed my eyes and stayed quiet, hoping he'd go back to bed.

In the morning I asked Banner why he'd gotten up.

"I just wanted to give you and Dad a hug and tell you I love you."

Adam had received his hug, but I had missed mine.

Conviction.

The Lord used this incident to teach me something—not to condemn me but to graciously reveal a truth about His character that I forget. Often I feel as if God is mad or disappointed because I haven't been good enough or haven't done enough. I assume that He wants to interrupt my well-oiled agenda and have me do something else, something more. Yet, like Banner, He impressed this on me: *What if I just want to tell you I love you? What if I want to wake you and tell you how crazy I am about you? You assume the worst, but what if I just want to spend time with you and remind you of My love?*

Revelation. What if God wasn't asking me to be Mary but instead loved me for being Martha?

It is interesting that Banner is the one whom God used to reveal this—

the son whose name is a continual reminder of this very idea. "He has brought me to his banquet hall, and his banner over me is love" (Song of Solomon 2:4, NASB).

Jesus sings love over us, whether we are standing, sitting, or sleeping. He displays His affection like a banner. He invites us to unwind in His presence and relax in His care. Although we need sleep, we can experience spiritual rest even when we are awake, even while we are working.

For years I've felt guilty for being task oriented. I scold myself for being a doer and then try to improve myself in five easy steps. The thing is, not only are the steps difficult, but they are pretty near impossible. I didn't choose to be a doer; I was designed to be one. This temperament—this nature—is here to stay. It's not to be erased but rather to be celebrated and used for God's glory. Just because we are designed to do doesn't mean we are inferior or su-perior to Mary types.

There is nothing wrong with being like Martha or Mary. Both are cre-ated by and loved by God. Praise Jesus for both kinds of women! I enjoy my Mary friends. They help me slow down and stay focused on what is truly important when my to-do list threatens to derail my joy. However, I'm equally thankful for my Martha friends. They are my go-to gals for getting things done. One of these friends recently came over and cleaned my fridge until it shone like the top of the Chrysler Building. *Glory!*

Dangerous Additives

Way back in the Garden of Eden, Satan caused doubt to ring in the ears of sister Eve when he questioned and twisted what God had lovingly instructed about not eating the fruit from the tree of the knowledge of good and evil (see Genesis 3:1–3). With his words Satan crafted a picture of a God who was holding out on His daughter. Eve also added to what God said (by telling the serpent that the fruit couldn't even be touched), kind of like the Judaizers of Jesus's day, who added extra rules to the rules (which bred pride and rebellion).

Satan has done similar things with doers like us. He has exploited this familiar passage about Mary and Martha in Luke 10:38–42 to convince God's doer daughters that our wiring is flawed, causing us to doubt we are wonderfully made. The accuser of our souls has spun these five verses in Scripture to imply that we are not fully loved or acceptable unless we become someone else, someone more. We have bought into the lie that we are supposed to improve on this God-given design because it isn't as adored as Mary's is. But this is not true!

Jesus never asked Martha to be Mary, and He didn't ask you to be either. He simply pointed out that you do not have to serve from a place of striving and worry, because He is already enough for you. He is not holding out on you. We have added words to what Jesus said and have compromised parts of who He created us to be in the process. Enough is enough! Pointing out one behavior to improve on is not the same as criticizing the totality of who you are. Let's stop agreeing with the serpent and others who echo his slippery sentiments.

Let's not view this passage in Luke as condemnation but as an invitation to freedom. Let's stand together, confident in who we are and who we belong to. Our doing isn't the problem. But our motivation for doing is where things get messy. And we aren't a fan of messes, are we?

Jesus lovingly reminds us of the importance of receiving, not just doing. He invites us to breathe deeply with the lungs He's laced together.

So let's pause. Here at the beginning, let's take a deep, cleansing breath—the in-through-the-top-of-our-heads-and-out-through-the-bottom-of-our-toes kind.

When was the last time you received the love of the Lord, no strings attached, without condition? Rest for a moment, right here amid the mess. Tune in to guilt-free grace, singing a lullaby to your hardworking heart.

Modern Martha Mandy Scarr

[My daughter's] middle name is Abigail. It means "my father's joy." Together [my husband and daughter] have begun to teach me of the Father's unconditional love in ways no one else has ever been able to speak into my heart. The way he looks at her, the way he cherishes her, the way he protects her. The way she finds peace and comfort in his arms ... home even. He's that way with [our son] too—nothing is really that different, but there is just something there between this girl and her Daddy that goes deeper. Their relationship, it's feeding her soul. Being a witness to their love is beautiful for a girl like me, a girl who struggles to understand the vastness of my heavenly Father's love towards me; a girl who wrestles with understanding His perfect fulfillment of the role of Father in my life because of wounds and scars and pain associated with that title. ... Together they are teaching me what my soul longs to hear ... that I am my Father's joy, just as I am, exactly as He made me. Oh how my heart hungers to know this at its core with unfailing belief. I am my Father's joy and the apple of His eye. And guess what ... so are you, beloved. So are you.[2]

☐ It Is Finished: For You

There is much to be done each day. Take a few moments to jot down what's currently stressing you out.

Although there are many things to do, the greatest to-do has already been completed. Read Isaiah 53 and John 19:28–30 and record what Jesus has accomplished on your behalf.

2

The Worry-and-Worship Conflict

Laying Down "What If" and Lifting Up "Even If"

❧

> I love that image of Christ replacing worry at the
> center of my life. With Christ at the center, our
> minds are settled and our hearts are at rest. We
> know God is working everything for good.
>
> —**Betsy de Cruz**, *Faith Spilling Over* (blog)

*B*ecause I'm a doer by design, each day brings me new challenges to
conquer—on the good days. On the bad days, it all feels over-
whelming and I'm tempted to hide under warm covers. Frantic thoughts rob
me of joy and steal peace. *What if I forget something? What if I lose my
temper? What if I don't have what it takes? What if "IT" happens?*

Worry is often my default emotion. I wonder how everything will turn
out and try to prepare myself for whatever might come. My war with worry
often attacks my resolve to live with open hands and a clear mind. I try to
solve the world's problems, or at least those that pound on my front door, and
I'm left discouraged. I bypass peace while marching toward self-reliance. I

strategize so I won't be capsized by the unexpected. I long for victory, for an end to my fretting, yet I keep walking along the familiar path of anxious living.

I posed this question to a variety of women on Facebook: "What are some things you worry about on a regular basis?" Their answers poured in quickly: "what others think of me," "health issues," "not being enough for my kids," "being harmed," "not being able to pay rent," "how to get everything done," "failing miserably as a follower of Christ," "not doing what I was made to do." One of them said, "Sadly, I have a PhD in worrying."

Jesus reveals that Martha was worried and bothered by many things too. I'll bet that Martha was also a what-if woman. *What if there's not enough food for the party? What if my to-do list is longer than the time I have? What if I'm left alone to do all the work? What if? What if?*

Why do we worry? Could it be because of fear, past hurts, difficult circumstances, unrealistic expectations, or a lack of trust? Or maybe we think we don't have enough for what might be required. Or maybe we don't think we are enough for what we might face. Or we wonder whether God is enough.

After I conducted my informal survey about why women worry, my friend sent this quote: "Worry is believing God won't get it right."[1] Whoa. That sounds extreme, but isn't that what I communicate when I allow worry to overshadow the promises and power of God? I abandon confidence in the Faithful One as I seek comfort from my familiar companion—Worry.

THE WEIGHT OF WORRY

During my final year of college, I lived in an apartment about a mile from campus. I walked to school so I wouldn't have to buy a parking permit. Since I didn't have much of a break between classes, I hauled the whole day's supply of textbooks and notebooks with me from class to class. The campus was in the middle of Michigan, so often my fluffy red coat went on before I heaved my lead-weight backpack on top of it. My pack jutted out like an iceberg as I hurried to campus, late as usual.

One day my friend (now husband) Adam drove by as I was half jogging, half hobbling to class. He teased me later, saying I looked like a puffy marshmallow with a turtle shell on my back. I laugh now, realizing how ridiculous I looked, bent over from the weight of my protruding backpack. I wanted to be prepared for anything and equipped with everything I might need, yet I could hardly stand up under the weight of it all.

Sometimes worry feels like a heavy backpack, causing hunched posture and inhibiting forward motion. Wringing hands, a furrowed brow, and rhythmic pacing accompany worry as we face the unknown. Worry can cause us to stumble, as we doubt that God will come through. It can keep us tethered to the what-ifs and now-whats. And it can trip us as we limp around, trying to uphold what is ill fitting and cumbersome.

My friend Kris has firsthand experience with worry, and it holds her back from walking in freedom. She was filled with concern that the residents at the adult-care facility where she works wouldn't like her food. She allowed doubts about her abilities to slip in. That fear had a profound effect: Kris admitted that nothing she makes tastes good to her when she is in a state of worry. She loses her appetite, finds smells nauseating (ones that should be good!), and needs to bring in her coworkers to determine whether her food tastes okay because she just can't tell.

Kris also noticed that when she was consumed with worry, she dropped things, made messes, and added too much or too little of something. Even things as simple as covering a tray with plastic wrap became difficult. Her desire to please others was so overpowering that it backfired. She tried to control situations that were out of her control, but she realized, "Some people just won't like liver and onions, no matter what you do to that dish!" Kris hated the idea of letting people down with a bad meal. She became aware that she took this simple act she'd performed for her family every day for decades and made it into a complicated ordeal. She knew that the only solution was to seek God's help. When she began to rely on Him—to pray and worship while cooking—real change came. She recognized how fear was affecting both her confidence and her ability and that she was being rendered powerless.

Worry is something Kris still struggles with to a degree, but she is purposeful in facing it. Just the other night, she was concerned about making peach pie for the first time. Her initial impression of the finished product was that the crust was underbaked, so she asked her administrator to try a bite. She loved it! Kris went for a second taste and realized it was good—very good, in fact. As worry melted away, her taste buds revived.

For us women who try to handle it all, worry is a common coping strategy, but it's in conflict with the antidote at our disposal. Worry suffocates worship. As we spin our wheels and head nowhere fast, it keeps us from resting within and from the very thing that can fill us with sweet peace.

Martha found herself in a similar place. It seems she was so consumed with cares that she forgot the One who is most careful with her. She was so focused on her works that she missed the Worthy One in her midst: Jesus, the water-to-wine miracle worker, the feed-the-five-thousand supernatural provider, the raise-the-dead anointed healer.

Have I, like Martha, overlooked the One who resides in the home of my heart? Have worrying and being overly responsible crippled my faith? Have the what-ifs distracted me from the I AM?

I think so.

Now, there was much more to Martha than worry. We know she was beloved, created by God, and a friend of Jesus. She was hospitable and capable too, although her worth did not stem from those things. Jesus did not ask

Martha to ignore the needs of others, nor did He discount her work ethic and tendency to be responsible. He asked her to take notice and recognize who He was (Love) and who she was as a result (beloved).

With kindness, Jesus speaks through our striving—straight to our hearts. He invites us to find Him, buried beneath the burden of working to be enough.

Somewhere along the way, we have exchanged the good news of grace for a proving and earning lifestyle. I started out believing His love, but then I tried to keep it by doing more and more. And as I did more, I worried more: *What if it isn't enough? What if I can't keep up? What if I mess up?* I kept trying to one-up so that I would measure up. I feared the disappointment of others and God, so I strove to be worthy. The Law and additional rules around it, coupled with self-effort, were armed guards to keep me in line. I worked myself into a prison cell of performance, as if it all depended on me. The straining to be worthy resulted in soul fatigue.

There had to be a better way.

I would soon find it, but it wasn't a result of trying harder.

FIRST LINE OF DEFENSE

As I labored over the words of this chapter, I grew anxious. I aspired to be a wordsmithing wizard, yet my words fell flat. I worked hard to inspire but came up short. I was trying to encourage others to worship instead of worry—only I worried as I wrote.

At church on a Sunday soon after this worry fest, God gently uncovered my hypocrisy. During a song I shook my head and laughed quietly, realizing the error of my ways. Hands lifted, unencumbered, I worshipped. With my voice I declared God's goodness, trusting that He would bring the words in His timing. Through His kind prodding, I laid down my burdens and lifted my voice and hands to the Holy One. My worry dissipated as dependence was communicated. My perspective changed, even though my circumstances had not. God reminded me of His goodness and faithfulness and that my best efforts wouldn't redeem the situation as only He can.

It reminded me of a time I had to make a difficult phone call to a friend. There had been a misunderstanding, and I feared the backlash that would most likely ensue. I drove home from a retreat, getting ready to call this friend to try to clear the air. At this women's retreat near the shores of Lake Michigan, author and speaker Annie Downs encouraged us to worship even in dark times, as Paul and Silas did from their jail cell (see Acts 16:22–30).[2] They had been accused, beaten, and incarcerated. From their inner cell, with feet fastened in stocks, they began to pray and sing to God. There was a violent earthquake, and the foundation of the prison was shaken. All the prison doors flew open, and everyone's chains came loose (see verse 26). Not only were Paul and Silas set free, but also the jailer, and his household, came to the Lord through this miraculous turn of events.

The prisoners could have remained stuck, weighed down by worry, but instead, worship set them free. Their brows weren't furrowed; their eyes were fixed on Jesus. They weren't wringing their hands; they were singing. They demonstrated a posture of trust despite finding themselves in a dark place. They communicated confidence in their Savior, even in chains.

In 2 Chronicles 20, we read about another time present circumstances seemed hopeless and incessant worry would have been a natural response.

King Jehoshaphat faced a "vast army" in battle: "We have no power to face this vast army that is attacking us. We do not know what to do, but our eyes are on you" (verse 12, NIV).

Instead of trying to attack the problem on their own, the people "came together to seek help from the LORD" (verse 4, NIV). Then the Spirit of the Lord came on a man named Jahaziel "as he stood in the assembly" (verse 14,

NIV), and part of his message was "Do not be afraid or discouraged because of this vast army. For the battle is not yours, but God's. . . . You will not have to fight this battle. Take up your positions; stand firm and see the deliverance the LORD will give you, Judah and Jerusalem. Do not be afraid; do not be discouraged. Go out to face them tomorrow, and the LORD will be with you" (verses 15, 17, NIV).

King Jehoshaphat responded by appointing men to sing to the Lord and go out ahead of the army. He sent the worshippers out first, and a supernatural event transpired: "As they began to sing and praise, the LORD set ambushes against the men of Ammon and Moab and Mount Seir who were invading Judah, and they were defeated" (verse 22, NIV).

The people were worried, but they went to the Lord. This was so much more than singing; it was an act of surrendering. They declared God's goodness and proclaimed His power, and while they did, He fought for them. The Lord was with them, and the enemy was defeated. *Glory!*

I decided to try to do the same thing. What was there to lose? Before I dialed my friend's number, the one who was angry with me over the misunderstanding, I worshipped. At first it felt awkward, but as I acknowledged God, peace rose.

What if the phone call goes poorly? Well, even if it does, God is still in charge and still able to do the impossible. Assurance silenced worry as I summoned trust and belief in the mightiness of God. I did not have to work myself up to make something happen. I reminded myself of who He already was. The results were up to Him, but hope was available, even amid uncertainty. My soul settled down as my confidence in God grew.

Thankfully, the phone call went much better than expected. But even if it hadn't, my mind would have been renewed as I remembered the power of God and acknowledged the presence of His Spirit. Worship released me from the tight grip of worry.

My friend Amy Elaine shared a powerful vision that God gave her of what this worry/worship transfer might look like in the spiritual realm:

> I come to Him with my hands tied behind my back. As I begin to declare His goodness, He unravels me. No longer bound, I am free. Grabbing hold of the strings of my heart, I lasso the thoughts and worries swirling around me. Now, it's true, I am an Oklahoma girl, but it wasn't until moving to Colorado that I went to my first rodeo. Watching real-life cowboys in action is a sight to see as they hurl their ropes with precision and catch their prize. . . .
>
> You see, if we'll let Him, God can teach us how to take down every stronghold that threatens our intimacy with Him. We, too, can catch our prize.
>
> "We are demolishing arguments and ideas, every high-and-mighty philosophy that pits itself against the knowledge of the one true God. We are taking prisoners of every thought, every emotion, and subduing them into obedience to the Anointed One" (2 Corinthians 10:5, Voice).
>
> Making declarations of His goodness easily unties the knots and loosens the grip of the world. With God on our side, we become excellent ropers, using the very ties that bound us to lasso in our freedom.[3]

I love this picture of God helping us lasso lies by actively applying His truth. We take our concerns to Him, and He meets us there in our place of need.

In Daniel 3, Shadrach, Meshach, and Abednego faced a fiery furnace in Babylon because they would not bow to King Nebuchadnezzar's image of gold (talk about a big worry!). Yet they declared, "If we are thrown into the blazing furnace, the God we serve is able to deliver us from it, and he will deliver us from Your Majesty's hand. But even if he does not, we want you to know, Your Majesty, that we will not serve your gods or worship the image of gold you have set up" (verses 17–18, NIV).

May our "what if" worry be changed to "even if" worship as we remember who is with us. Even if our what-if happens, the good news does not change. Jesus is enough, even in the dark, even in the battle, even among flames.

I don't know about you, but I've wasted enough time worrying. I'm ready to trade in my foggy thinking for a clear view of the gospel. I want to experience the foundation of the prison shaking and the doors flying open as everyone's chains fall off! I want to see the Enemy defeated as we let God fight for us, as we stand firm on His promises. I want to see Jesus dancing in the fire with us as we refuse to bow down to another. I want to learn to sit instead of throwing a fit when things don't turn out as expected.

We don't have to be prisoners of worry, even if we're faced with confining circumstances. Let's retire from it and choose to trust our Creator, Savior, and Sustainer—not as a last resort but as a first line of defense.

My friend Niki (who has a fabulous British accent) prayed for me to choose worship over worry because of an unsettling doctor's appointment for one of my kids. She prayed that my child would hunger for food and that I would hunger for God at every turn. She went on to say something that made an enormous difference in how I approach worry: "Where fear and worry are appetizing, may she grow sick of that. May worship and Your Word be more fulfilling and appetizing than worry."

We starve worry by not sneaking it scraps under the table. We don't let it grow rapidly in size, because we refuse to feed it. Instead of being manipulated by worry, we divert our attention to worship. We take our hunger to God and ask Him to strengthen and satisfy us as we feast on truth.

JUST ONE THING

In the same way Jesus reclined in the home of Mary and Martha, He tenderly speaks to us from His residence in our hearts. He answers our what-if with Himself.

My daughter, what if your limp turned to lightness because of one thing? What if your striving became settledness because of just one thing? What if your frantic turned to freedom through one thing alone?

"Wait, what? Just one thing? Remember how I get bored when there's not much to do? On the other hand, I also get worn out when I try to do everything. But explain Yourself, Lord. What do You mean? It sounds too good to be true, almost too easy for a doer like me."

You are worried and bothered about so many things, but only one thing is necessary.

"Excuse me, Lord, but how can You narrow it down to just one thing? I mean, there's Bible study, there's prayer (which I'm pretty lousy at), there's ministry, there's communion on the first Sunday of the month, don't get me started on fasting, there's a house to clean, there's laundry that never seems to get folded (but I swear it's clean; it's just in piles), there's—"

I love you.

"Thanks, Jesus. I really appreciate that, but . . . here comes the *but*, right?"

My daughter . . .

"Yes, Lord, I'm listening. Well, I'm trying to listen, but do You see those stray pieces of cereal that didn't get swept up over there?"

It's taken care of. It's done.

"What? The sweeping?"

Oh, my darling, no, but what you are striving for is already settled. I loved you in your mess, in the midst of your sin. I left the majesty of heaven to come to earth as a baby. I lived a sinless life. I was killed as a spotless Lamb for your sins and rose again. I finished what God sent Me to accomplish.

I came to your house and you willingly welcomed Me. You opened the door and invited Me in. But over time you have forgotten who I am. Your worrying has run you right past the Worthy One. You have overlooked the fact that I reside within your heart and am not going anywhere. Nothing you do or don't do will change My love for you.

I'm here to stay.

You don't have to clean up for Me—cereal or character.

You are enough because I am enough. You are declared complete because I have completed the work, once and for all. You are free to sit, stand, work, and rest because of what I have accomplished on the cross. It is done!

The one thing for you to do is rest within because I have removed your sin. It's an extravagant gift called grace, and it's yours. It's the one thing.

I AM the one thing.

"Whoa. I can stop striving because You cleaned the mess of sin, once and for all? I've made it so complicated. I've tried to obtain and keep what is already mine through a lot of sweat and tears. I have added heavy burdens to myself and others when it was no longer necessary."

Only one thing is necessary, and I already did it. Your part is to believe and receive. Rest in grace. You won't get bored. Take off that ill-fitting backpack full of self-imposed burdens and unwrap grace instead. Grace was costly, but I offer it to you as a gift, no strings attached, without guilt or condemnation.

My yoke is easy and My burden is light. I am gentle and humble in heart, and you will find rest for your soul.

Fresh oxygen fills my lungs. Salvation does not depend on us!

We rest within. We don't have to earn approval!

We can keep doing, but it's no longer a means to gain worth.

Yes, we will sweep cereal. Yes, we will take care of others. Yes, we will offer our best. But the sweeping, the caring, and the offering are not what bring us closer to or keep us from Jesus.

The antidote for worry is belief—pure, uncomplicated belief. The "Jesus loves me—this I know, for the Bible tells me so"[4] kind of belief.

EASY STREET

Do you stumble over this one thing—this grace thing? Do you try to pick it up and strap it on, but it slips through your fingers, just out of reach? It feels too simple, too light, so you bend down and pick up the ever-so-familiar "Law log" to try to keep yourself in line. It's weighty from the pressure to be perfect, with all its dos and don'ts etched on it (see Galatians 3:23–24). You heave the log onto your back and start to walk under its strain. It is uncomfortable and heavy, but at least you know where you stand. At times, you pile on extra weight, either as punishment or as pride—depending on how you're feeling—as you grunt and groan your way forward. Not far down the road, your back starts to ache from trying to uphold the Law in your own strength. You stop for a moment and wonder whether it could really be true. Could God want you "as is"? Could His "already did" really be enough? Could His grace really be free and emancipate you from striving, at last?

Maybe, just maybe, there is a different way to be outfitted for this journey. No, it doesn't require more weight on your back, but it calls for you to hand over what you've relied on for so long. At times, you feel disoriented and clumsy as you learn to walk differently. Sometimes you will go back for that log, but as you grasp grace, the turning back will lessen as you walk further down the Freedom Trail.

Jesus is enough. Period.

Worry is replaced by worship (a reverent trust and grateful adoration of God), not because you try harder (nor because you try harder to *not* try harder) but because you are assured that you don't have to! Can you hear the liberty bells clanging? Is it really this easy? Is the good news truly this good?

For decades, I attempted to perfect myself and I was miserable. My mind was cluttered, trying to sort out law versus grace. My shoulders ached from the pressure of having to prove myself. I was easily offended as I held others to the unrealistic standard that I labored to achieve. Anger was my automatic emotion as the beat of expectations stomped lightheartedness. Then I found what I had lost along the way: the easy yoke of grace, the light burden of belief.

I was both overjoyed and embarrassed at this discovery. How did I, a Christian since I was a child, miss the main thing? The seeds had been planted along the way, but it wasn't until my fortieth birthday neared that the conflict of law versus grace was resolved between head and heart. I felt born again—born into an inheritance that wouldn't spoil, fade, or perish based on my behavior. I started reading the Word once more, not because I had to but because grace lenses brought the good news into focus. No longer heard as chiding, Jesus's gentle voice of love filled my ears. It was the difference between reading kind words on a birthday card and bad marks on a report card.

Wringing our hands, furrowing our brows, and pacing with worry are no longer the posture required since the Law was fulfilled through Jesus. The Holy One answered the ultimate worry with Himself. His nailed hands, punctured brow, and total sacrifice on the cross made a way for us to be reborn.

As we tune into His love, the scolding silences. Our posture changes when we realize we are adored. Our eyes sparkle when we know we have the affection of another. Our heads clear when we believe what's already true.

Exchanging Worry for Worship

When we fixate on the what-ifs, it's as though we're trying to navigate through a dense forest. We try to get around obstacles and anticipate potential threats, and we expend a great deal of energy in the process. Our bodies and emotions are fatigued from constantly being on high alert. We try to clear a path through the briars, yet we find ourselves stuck in the thick of it. We need a perspective change or we'll be tempted to despair in our tangled state.

As we allow the skilled Gardener to cut away the stubborn roots with His pruning shears of truth, we can be released from the cyclical thoughts that hold us back. We turn the key that locks up worry and unlocks worship, as we remember who He is and who we are in light of Him. Our point of view shifts, our thinking clears, and we find comfort even in the middle of demands, detours, and deadlines.

Following are the keys to helping us exchange worry for worship.

1. Recount the characteristics of God.

As you read Scripture, keep an ongoing list of what you learn about God. Record the references next to the characteristics so you can refer to them quickly. For example, in Psalm 103, you learn that

- the Lord is worthy of praise (verse 1)
- His name is holy (verse 1)
- His benefits are to be remembered (verse 2)
- He forgives all your sins (verse 3)
- He heals you (verse 3)
- He lifts you up from the pit (verse 4)
- He shows you compassion and love (verse 4)
- He satisfies you with good things (verse 5)

As you focus on God's specific attributes, your worry melts away in contrast to the magnitude of His greatness. Revisit your list and add to it as you read the Bible. Ask the Holy Spirit to write these characteristics of God on your heart and bring them to mind, especially as you face "what if" and "now what" moments.

2. Recall specific promises of God.

Ask God to give you a specific scripture to stand on to help you stay grounded in truth as you face worrisome situations. For example, when my husband and I were waiting to adopt a child, the promise of Galatians 6:9 was like an intravenous line of hope, sustaining us through uncertainty: "Let us not grow weary of doing good, for in due season we will reap, if we do not give up."

Are you tempted to throw in the towel and walk out that door because you're tired of doing good? Are you bound by anxious thoughts as you face the future? Are you weary from trying to meet all the demands pressing in on you? Me too. Even the most devoted doers get discouraged when the end to their task is nowhere in sight or proves beyond their capabilities. We need to tap into a power greater than our own—to remember the character and the benefits of belonging to our heavenly Father.

As we recall the specific promises of God, our belief strengthens and our resolve rises. The ground beneath us becomes a solid foundation as we stand on truth.

3. Remember God's faithfulness in the past.

In an awesome display of power, God parted the Red Sea for the Israelites as they fled Egypt and Pharaoh's approaching army (see Exodus 14). He also caused the Jordan River to be cut off (at flood stage) as His people miraculously crossed over on dry ground again. After the whole nation crossed the river, God told Joshua to have twelve men, one from each tribe, take up twelve stones from the middle of the Jordan. These stones were to serve as signs of God's power and faithfulness, helping them and their children (and us) remember the great things God had done (see Joshua 4:7, 20–24).

When we find ourselves facing the floodwaters of worry, let's pause and ask God to help us remember His faithfulness. In what specific ways has He already come through for you (from salvation to sustenance, from shelter to support)? Reflect on your own life and also the accounts found in Scripture where God demonstrates that He is indeed the way maker, the sea parter, the wave walker. As we revisit our memorial stones, our worry dissipates and our worship intensifies.

4. Release the situation to God's keeping.

Remembering God's faithfulness from the past brings comfort, but sometimes our present circumstances cause us to clench our fists (whether shaking them at God or grasping for the reins of control). When what-ifs become harsh reality, we may be tempted to tackle Jordan River–sized worries on our own. But we can release our fears into the depths of His sufficiency. We are not designed to strap the cares of this world onto our backs and lug them around. We are instructed to cast our cares on the Capable One as He leads us through.

The word *cast* is an interesting one. Picture a fisherman casting his line out into the waters, away from himself. A transfer of energy happens. And that is what we can do with our concerns as well. We don't just try to stop worrying; we actively cast our worries on Jesus.

5. Rest in who you are in Christ.

Like Martha, we may get bogged down with all there is to do and then stress about how everything will turn out. Yet as we recount who God is, recall His promises, remember His faithfulness, and release our cares to Him, we learn to rest in who we are in Christ. We belong to Him and we are loved by Him. And the best part? Even in our worry, He is crazy about us. *Even if* we never make it through these five steps, Jesus has already passed through to make a way for our hearts. We leave behind worry and step into worship as we follow the lead of the One to whom we belong. We lean into God's character and capabilities, and our souls are invited to rest.

Modern Martha Nicole Homan

Worship starts with relationship. "We love because he first loved us" (1 John 4:19). We encounter the reality of His love, and it is from that place that we worship. Worship is extravagant love and respect for an object of esteem. Worship should not be about trying to get, earn, or prove something. Worship is simply loving God back. First John 3:1 tells us, "See what kind of love the Father has given to us, that we should be called children of God." We get to call Him Father. He paid for our adoption with the blood of His firstborn Son. Our name is carved into His palm. How can you not be crazy about that kind of Daddy? How can we not worship?[5]

☐ It Is Finished: Even If!

Write down some of the what-ifs you worry about.

Write down some "even if" statements that assure you of who God is despite circumstances. Read Psalms 103 and 136 to remind you of who He is and what He does.

3

These Shoulders

The Heavy Load That Dependable Daughters Carry

∽

I could hold you for a million years
To make you feel my love

—Bob Dylan, "Make You Feel My Love"

The earthy fragrance of lavender oil permeates the air as my friend Tami and I enter the room for our massages. We are attending a women's retreat and have chosen the "relaxing" free-time option, as opposed to zip-lining or braving the high-ropes course. Our massages are during the same time slot, with two different masseuses; however, the only thing separating us is a flimsy partition. It is difficult to withhold giggles as I hear my friend's masseuse karate chopping her back. *Thwack, thwack, thwack!* We have a good laugh afterward.

As I lie there on the massage table, the sweet gal working on my back reminds me to relax. It has been a difficult time in ministry, and my shoulders are especially tense from carrying stress. When you tell a type A woman to relax, *she strives to do it.* Here lies the paradox: we work to relax. It's not that we totally mind relaxing, but we often labor to get there. We put a check mark by it on our to-do list: Yep, I did it. I relaxed!

Relaxing doesn't come naturally unless we are done with all we planned on accomplishing for the day (and that list is not short and is often unrealistic). It's as if this thought perches on our shoulders, bearing down with a heavy weight: "If only you could check everything off your list, you could relax and be at peace. But the more you work to accomplish that goal, the more things crop up on your list. The harder you try, the more frustrated you become."[1]

As I try to release the tension from my shoulders on the massage table, I realize that even when I rest, it's hard to unwind.

NOT MINE TO CARRY

Not long after this massage realization, a greater revelation comes during a conversation with an older woman I will call Denise. In her fifties, Denise is facing health problems and believes that part of the reason for this is many years of taking on "responsibilities" that really weren't hers. She explains that when we "play God" in others' lives—thinking we know best how to help and fix things—we are doing the Holy Spirit's job. This is blasphemy.

As I listen to Denise talk, a thick curtain falls, and I can clearly see what I have been doing for years. Denise shares her struggles and sheds light on mine too, calling our shared hang-ups *sin*, for that's what they really are. She speaks a timely word in the gentlest of ways and I start to get it. Because of my ultraresponsible approach, I have taken on things that aren't mine to carry. I am weighed down with trying to play the Holy Spirit and take care of things that are outside the territory He has given me.

Denise encourages me to ask God when all this started. As I stand there, silently asking God to show me, He quickly impresses this on my heart:

"When you were two and a half." *Two and a half? Really, God? Why then?* And as soon as the thought spills out, the answer comes. That was when my brother was born—my endearing, sweet brother, Brian, who has Down syndrome. I don't remember anyone asking or expecting me to, but I believe that's when I started carrying things that were not mine to lift—scooping up control for fear of being caught off guard or falling apart.

Prepared. Vigilant. Able. A little soldier of sorts, armed with self-sufficiency.

In her book *Grace for the Good Girl*, Emily Freeman talks about having a responsible mind-set like Martha's (and like mine): "I see myself as irreplaceable when I think that the work won't get done unless I do it. Instead of looking to him to provide what is needed, Martha rolled up her sleeves and took on responsibility for things that may never have been meant for her."[2]

Martha seemed to work first, then relax afterward. She probably waited until the task was done and *then* sat down to enjoy those around her. *Can I get a witness?* Maybe she, like me, had yet to learn how to really enjoy people's company while completing a line item. Maybe she, like me, had yet to learn how to rest within, secure in her position as a dear daughter of God.

It is a good thing to be reliable, but there is a sneaky shift that can happen from being responsible to putting ourselves in charge of things that aren't ours to manage.

I tried to mother my siblings when my mom was already doing just fine. I tried to control things and make them happen as I wanted, trying to be the god of my own universe. I wore these characteristics proudly, like a sash, declaring, "I'm Miss Conscientious from the University of Dependability. You can count on me. I'm reliable and able to get things done." I took pride in how responsible I was, but after Denise's disclosure and exhortation, I began seeing this behavior as something to be refined and adjusted and sometimes even confessed as sin. I witnessed the long-term consequences that this way of life can wage on someone's health and well-being, and I want to change course.

I need to let go and lay down the things that aren't mine, such as parenting my brother. I am Brian's sister, not his mother, so I want to start enjoying him as a brother. And the tough stuff we were dealing with in ministry? I needed to let God take care of that too. Through Denise's words, I began to envision the freedom that could be mine if I chose to trust God to work as He saw fit.

When you stop trying to fix everyone and everything around you, you begin to experience joy and peace in a deeper way. God may ask you to carry heavy things at times, but let's not willingly pick up things that weren't meant for our shoulders. Jesus's shoulders are able to withstand the weight of the world. He cares for and leads us with unconditional, unending love. When we enter into covenant with Him—meaning a loving and abiding relationship with Him, through faith in who He is and what He has done—He promises to provide us with what we need. Jesus takes on our debt, our insufficiency, all that we lack. He lovingly straps on the slack as He chooses to take care of us.

When I act independently of Christ and erect walls around my heart, it is often because I have a skewed view of who He is.

On His Watch

Often I think I know better than God does. I don't dare say it out loud, of course, but my actions communicate, "I know what should be done in this situation. I know what's best. If I only say or do this, then these people will see the light and change their behavior" (according to what I want them to do). But there is one Sovereign who reigns over all (see Psalm 103:19), one named El Roi, the God Who Sees.

Some of us don't want God looking in our direction. We assume that His gaze equates disapproval, as if He is watching like a hawk, just waiting for us to slip up so He can swoop down and lecture us or punish us.

Our management style at work or our parenting style at home might mirror that of "I'm watching to make sure you are doing everything right." I am afraid this is how my children feel most of the time. But to change, I need to understand how my heavenly Father relates to me on this side of the Cross.

In second grade, I tried out for the musical *Annie* at a nearby community theater. At my audition, I sang with gusto and hand motions. Much to my delight, I got a callback. At the second audition, I had to learn a dance and sing a part of "It's the Hard-Knock Life." My grandparents and parents attended the audition, sitting in the back of the theater. Partway through the song, I made eye contact with them and buckled under pressure. I forgot the words and didn't make it into the show. I was humiliated and took it out on my parents, blaming them for being there. If they hadn't been watching, I might not have lost focus, I reasoned.

When I wasn't picked for the musical, I chose to view my parents' presence at the audition as an unwanted intrusion instead of proof of their loving support. They weren't hoping to see me fail. They loved me and were in my corner. They wanted me to succeed. Their gazes were of admiration, not condemnation. When I botched the audition, they showed empathy, not exasperation. When I didn't make the cut, I unfairly accused those who sacrificed for me to be there in the first place.

And I have done the same with God, more times than I care to admit. I get hurt, whether by my own doing, someone else's doing, or a fluke, and I blame my heavenly Father. *Why did You let this happen? Don't You care about me? You ask me to trust You, but You don't do things as I think You should.*

When we question His love, resent His watchful eye, or accuse Him of not being there for us, we exhibit an orphan mentality. We act as if His love is conditional, which is a depressing way to exist. We work as if it's all up to us, which is a tiring way to function. We keep Him at arm's length, which is a lonely way to live.

But even in spite of our dysfunctional cycle of self-preservation, our Father invites us to turn and see Him for who He is: a Father who delights in His children and wants them to succeed.

Yes, there are times for His correction, "for the LORD corrects those he loves, just as a father corrects a child in whom he delights" (Proverbs 3:12, NLT). But His discipline is driven by love. When He corrected Martha, it was for her good. He invited her to turn from an orphan mentality of *I am overlooked. I am forgotten. It's all up to me.* And He invited her to see that even among demands and pressures, she was a beloved daughter of a trustworthy Father. He looked on, not to keep her in line but because He enjoyed her, and He smiled as she utilized her strengths.

Like a father scooping up his child, delighting to show her affection, is God, who fathers us perfectly.

All my striving, all the responsibility I pride myself on hauling around like an overstuffed backpack, really translates to a trust issue: not really trusting that He is capable, not really believing that He's got this managing-the-universe-and-everyone-in-it thing down. Sure, I can trust Him with most of the world, but my small world? I'm not so sure. I want to have control of it and "help" those around me understand how things should work. But my way produces a bumper crop of irritation.

I need a better way, because the old let-me-handle-it-all approach is not delivering a harvest of tranquility within. What if there is a way for this weight to be lifted off these shoulders that were never made to haul around all this? *Yes, please!* What if there is a way to experience spiritual rest, whether I am working or relaxing, knowing that my position is settled in Christ? *Yes, and amen!*

As I acknowledge my inability to shoulder all this and that I'm not designed for it, I accept that Jesus is. What He did on the cross brings welcome release from our toil. He was sent to strap all our shortcomings and sins onto His shoulders. This truth causes me to admit that I don't have what it takes apart from Him. I'm dependent on Jesus to save me, and He's the only one capable of directing my life with all love and wisdom. I have to remind myself over and over that He is God and I am not.

You may resist this letting-God-be-responsible-for-you thing, but listen to what kind of Father He is:

> It was I who taught Ephraim to walk,
>> taking them by the arms;
> but they did not realize
>> it was I who healed them.
> I led them with cords of human kindness,
>> with ties of love.
> To them I was like one who lifts
>> a little child to the cheek,
>> and I bent down to feed them. (Hosea 11:3–4, NIV)

I need to let go of this lifestyle of striving or be crushed under the suffocating, impossible task of managing and directing people and circumstances I cannot control. My ties are often not cords of love but rather leashes that choke out life and limit those around me; I want them to be dependent on my wisdom so that I feel needed and secure.

With God's cords of human kindness and ties of love, He leads and guides, not to suffocate us but to help us release the tension as we walk freely in the knowledge of His sufficiency. As we relax our shoulders and open clenched fists, we communicate a posture of trust. Instead of dependence on what our hands can do, we yield to the One who made those hands, offering them as a tool to be lovingly guided and used by Him.

It's a good thing to be dependable. It is admirable to be able to manage many things and actively use our talents for the betterment of others. Working hard is not a bad thing! We, like Martha, are responsible for much, but when our attitude is unbalanced self-sufficiency or an unneeded, unwanted intrusion into the lives of those around us, we would be wise to reconsider our approach.

When we elevate our responsible behavior over God's ability to care for us—discounting His position and promoting our wills above His—we push back against the One who died to restore our rebellious hearts to the Father. We don't have to change in our own strength. Jesus is ready and willing to help—the head above our shoulders, the one able to carry us. He is more than qualified to bear our burdens.

THROUGH THE ROOF

His friends had been carrying him awhile. He was heavy. His problem weighed them down—not just physically but emotionally as well. They took his suffering seriously and they longed for a different outcome. They wanted to see their friend healed. But what could they do? If they could have taken away his pain, they would have. If they could have fixed his circumstances, they would have. If they could have restored his body, they would have. But they couldn't.

So they decided to take him to a physician who was growing in popularity. He was more of a nontraditional doctor, but they were desperate for a cure and open to unconventional methods. So they took their friend, by faith, to go and see this peculiar man. They hoped for a miracle.

When they reached their destination, there was a crowd blocking the door. But these determined friends removed a part of the roof and let down the pallet on which their friend, the paralytic, was lying (see Mark 2:4).

They made sure he made it to Jesus. And Jesus, seeing their faith, said to the paralytic, "Son, your sins are forgiven. . . . I say to you, get up, pick up your pallet and go home" (verses 5, 11, NASB).

Obviously, I took some liberty in retelling this Bible story from Mark 2, but I want to share it to explain a work that God did in my heart.

I was hauling a heavy burden. I was dragging around a dead-weight mummy, wrapped tightly in burial clothes. A few of my friends were crippled, spiritually speaking, and I was trying to shoulder their choices by lugging them around. This effort pulled me down physically and emotionally. I bowed my knees, begging God to set my friends free. I wrung my hands, furrowed my brow, and paced with worry, hunched over from this burden.

Then God reminded me of those who had brought their paralyzed friend to Jesus. They carried him, but only so they could lift him to Jesus, trusting Him to heal. They did what they could from a human stance and believed that Jesus would do what they could not.

I wept with relief as God asked me to lay down what I had been carrying.

It wasn't my place to be my friends' savior or to hold them up with my own strength. My part was to lift them to Jesus in prayer and let Him take it from there. As I raised my arms to reflect what He was showing me, I felt the weight lift. He took me from a place of pain and enabled me to rise up, limping no longer. I was not responsible for the outcome of my friends' choices. I entrusted them to the One who could make all the difference.[3]

Psalm 81:6–7 says,

I took the world off your shoulders,
    freed you from a life of hard labor.

You called to me in your pain;

    I got you out of a bad place. (MSG)

At first glance, I am hoping this verse is delivering us modern Marthas from having to do laundry and dishes anymore. Ha! Seriously, though, domestic dirty work is not the subject of this verse. The psalm points to the Hebrews' bondage in Egypt under the watchful eye of Pharaoh's slave masters: "[They] made their lives bitter with hard service, in mortar and brick, and in all kinds of work in the field. In all their work they ruthlessly made them work as slaves." (Exodus 1:14). God removed the yoke from their shoulders and freed His people from a life of slave labor.

Have you been serving a ruthless slave master, whether a false and graceless version of Jesus or the taskmaster of perfection concocted in an effort to prove worth? My dear Martha, you can be relieved of the weight you have been carrying. There may be laundry, dishes, and deadlines to tackle, yet the One who conquered sin and fulfilled the Law is able to deliver you from a life of bitter toil and bring you into a life of worshipful service.

The Burden Lifter speaks clear, gentle wisdom that realigns our thoughts with His truth. He removes our poor attempts at bandaging others and ourselves, and He works His healing salve into cracked places. He invites us to relate to Him as a slave no longer.

THE HIRED-HELP MENTALITY

It is important to evaluate why we do what we do. Yes, we are purposefully designed to be doers, yet there are times we use our doing as a means to cover up what lies beneath the surface. Some doers bury their hurts by staying busy. Others "do" in an effort to earn blessing. Yet avoidance and manipulation are the offspring of unbelief. Often issues such as control, insecurity, worry, proving, and even avoidance can be traced back to a lack of trust. At least that is the case for me, because if I really trusted God, wouldn't I be more at peace on the inside? If I really believed in His sufficiency, wouldn't I rest more easily? If I really took Him at His Word, wouldn't I be freed from fears?

Is this true of you? Do you feel as though God has let you down and so you work hard to look out for yourself?

A pastor's wife told me she felt God say to her, *I want you to take care of your family and also those sitting beside you.* She responded with something like "That's all fine and good, but who is going to take care of me?" God reassured her that He would.

Does His response reassure you? That He will take care of you and be responsible for you?

I sometimes struggle to believe this, mainly because I am not sure God will take care of me as I want Him to. He has proved Himself faithful time and time again, yet because circumstances have taken me by surprise on more than one occasion and there are situations in my life devoid of neat and tidy resolutions, I am skeptical.

And isn't that like big sister Eve? She believed the lie that God was holding out on her and that He wasn't completely trustworthy. She took matters into her own hands, in the form of forbidden fruit, and was wise in her own eyes, blinded to truth. I think she forgot she was a beloved daughter of a good Father. She reached out for something she did not have because her Father's boundary felt restrictive, not protective.

At the root of Eve's actions, there seems to be doubt in who God was and who she was in light of Him. Did Martha have her doubts too? Did Martha wonder who would take care of her since she was always taking care of others? Did she carry the weight of the world on her shoulders?

This mind-set of looking out for self and doubting the love of God is the motor that propels this way of thinking:

- I look out for myself because I question whether others will.
- I have a fear of missing out, and I think others are holding out on me.
- I am suspicious of people's motives and am easily offended by their actions.
- I have difficulty receiving because I am afraid that what is given will be taken away.
- I work hard so others won't find fault with me or reject me.
- I am vigilant about self-preservation and build walls to protect myself from hurt.
- I like to call the shots and am resistant to being told what to do.
- I have a hard time celebrating others because their success feels threatening.
- I try to get as much as I can for myself so I won't go without.
- I like to win because it makes me feel special and significant.

Another name for this mind-set is the orphan spirit, or an outlook of spiritual poverty. I also call it the hired-help mentality. It's the belief that you must earn your keep or else you might lose what you have.

After the conversation about taking on things I was not required to, Denise gave me some reading material about the orphan spirit. At first I was offended that she thought I exhibited this type of behavior (ironically, offense is a typical symptom of the orphan spirit). Because I grew up in a wonderful Christian home with loving and caring parents, I felt as though this whole orphan viewpoint did not add up. But then I recalled the self-imposed mantle of responsibility that I took on at a young age, and it started to make sense. I decided to look out for myself and call the shots, which translated into exerting control. I acted less like a daughter or sister and more like a mother hen, clucking and coercing, trying to be in charge and keep others in line.

Over time, my take-charge approach intensified and I didn't like who I had become. I barked orders and valued projects over people. I feared I was one bad decision away from losing the love of those closest to me. I lived as if it were up to me to keep the world in balance and make sure people were happy. On my quest to being enough for the Master and liked by others, I misplaced the joy of being a daughter.

DADDY'S ARMS

Martha is most often mentioned before her siblings in Scripture, so it is most likely that she was a firstborn, the older sister of Mary and Lazarus. That explains a lot. Firstborns are known for their heightened sense of responsibility. Luke 10:38 explains that the home Jesus visited belonged to Martha: "A woman named Martha welcomed Him into her home" (NASB). In the time in which they lived, it was rare for women to be unmarried. Therefore, there is speculation that Martha and Mary were orphaned (and not yet married), widows (who had not yet remarried), or possibly part of an ascetic Jewish sect that chose a life of singleness and celibacy. Any of these scenarios help us understand more about Martha and why she acted the way she did.[4]

It is also interesting to note that the Aramaic meaning of *Martha* is the feminine form of *lord* or *master,* likely a title of respect.[5] Her name embodies her responsible nature—of being a mother hen, if you will. (I knew I liked her.)

When Jesus corrected Martha for being distracted, worried, and bothered about so many things, He was more concerned about her heart and mind-set than her tasks and service. He did not discount her honorable service, yet He wanted her to understand she was a daughter first, delighted in by Him. She did not have to earn her place with all she could do or manage; she had value because God formed her in the womb. She had great worth, not because she could whip up the best batch of hummus around town or oversee her household well. Martha's worth came from the very One she welcomed into her home: Jesus. She had willingly received Him as an honored guest, yet He gave her an opportunity to receive from Him.

I wonder whether Martha had adopted a hired-help mentality over the years and had forgotten how to be a daughter—as I have, and many women I know, such as a woman I will call Nan:

I am an only child who grew up with a mom who battled sickness. Since about seven, I somehow decided that I was responsible for lots of things. Over the years, I kind of just skipped the daughter stage of life. I was always trying to be the one in charge—the one taking care of and nurturing others but lacking a nurture of my own.

As God healed me, I realized I had a big deficit. I didn't know how to receive comfort. I'm not sure I even really knew how to give it. I remember literally asking the Holy Spirit to comfort me and then something breaking in my heart as I felt His presence hover over and near me. He has told me many times that I may be uncomfortable but He will always comfort me. Now I run toward comfort. I ask for it. I lean into it. It's a little like water when you are thirsty.

I'm still being filled with those tender qualities I forsook in order to feel safe and in charge. I'm grateful He's allowing me to experience a bit of "childhood" even at my age.[6]

Several of my friends have admitted to me that they either don't feel like a daughter or don't quite know how to be one, whether through a strained relationship, the necessity of growing up quickly, or a personality bent. These are successful, smart, and hardworking women, yet circumstances such as family dynamics, distance, differences, expectations, loss, abandonment, and death contribute to a deficit in daughtership.

I am surprised to find myself among those women. I know how to earn and impress, but I don't really know how to receive and rest. I have soul fatigue from years of striving and I want to be made well.

So I pray, "Lord, teach me to be a daughter."

It's a little embarrassing for a forty-year-old woman with a healthy upbringing to admit this sort of thing. I feel as though I have made big strides in many aspects of my life, so it surprises me that I need to go back so far to go forward.

Sometimes in our grown-up attempts to keep it together, we cut off parts of who we are and live an amputated life. Sometimes we rush ahead and live disconnected from who we are at our core and bury what is most true of us. Sometimes our to-do lists don't leave room for the daughters in us.

To reclaim the daughter in me, I needed God to teach me to enjoy His presence.

"How do I do that, God?"

Do what you did as a child.

I had forgotten what it was like to be carefree, so I started making a list (because that's what this modern Martha likes to do), and it came back to me—the things I used to do as a little girl:

Swing as high as I could

Climb trees

Dance under the spotlight

Sing uninhibitedly

Use my hands to play, to create, and to orchestrate others

Enjoy food

Dress up in costumes

Do somersaults and cartwheels

Blow dandelion seeds off the stem

Pick flowers for my hair

Pose for photos

Make silly faces in the mirror

Laugh freely

Watch TV and eat popcorn

Type and write stories

Dream unedited

Ride my bike and let go of the handlebars

Hang out with friends

Gaze at clouds

Leave messes

Enjoy and anticipate celebrations and gifts

Trust my father to provide food, clothing, and shelter

Take my time

Go exploring

This list may bring a smile to your face, reminding you of a relatively carefree childhood, or it may stir up pain, particularly if your childhood was marked by stress, loss, or scars. Regardless of the nature of your upbringing, I believe that God can use simple acts like these—of enjoying life as a child—to help you uncover what it means to be His daughter.

It may be particularly challenging to embrace this idea if your earthly father let you down in profound ways. But what if you courageously viewed the hurt as an opportunity to illuminate what an attentive and loving Dad your heavenly Father is? When we focus on our heavenly Father instead of the failings of our earthly dads (or moms, for that matter), we begin to see God for who He is: a most capable and committed Father. Flawless. Always available. Just what we need.

The very God who breathed life into Eve, His first daughter, did not withhold love from her. And He is not holding out on us either. He has plenty of goodness to go around. He is able to give each of us His full attention. He doesn't tune us out or shoo us away. He does not rush us or make light of our pain but brings us close and holds us as dear daughters.

We depend on our Daddy to provide what we need—no neglect, no abuse, no betrayal, no abandonment. At the news that He is home, we race down the stairs into His embrace as He spins us around, glad to see us. We no longer fear the threat of "Wait until your Father gets home and hears what you did this time" because we know that although there are consequences for sin, He is a merciful Father, whose love and patience fuel His discipline. We trust His correction because He has proved His love for us. His delight in us is the foundation for our relationships with Him, not how many chores we completed or how well behaved we are. He loves us because we are His.

We take wobbly steps, then a running leap forward as we choose to trust the One who is most attentive to us. We see His smile, we hurry to meet His wide-open arms, and we learn what it means to be a daughter: a recipient of love.

Modern Martha Abby McDonald

I like to watch my kids when they don't know I'm looking.

I eavesdrop on interactions between firstborn and little brother. I overhear whispers of imagination, hide-and-seek and Legos.

It's not because I'm trying to catch them doing something wrong. On the contrary, I catch glimpses of their lives I might otherwise miss....

I'm a witness to these lives I helped create, and I love seeing them discover new things....

[But] somewhere along the line, I forgot God watches me with the love of a Father instead of an angry parent waiting to punish me. He sees me as a beloved daughter and a new creation, not a messed up kid who can't ever get anything right....

If I see my kids with the joy of a mother's heart, I know he sees me with a joy that surpasses my understanding. I know because the same God who created them created me. He created you. . . .

I want to smile back at God with the confidence of a daughter. A daughter who knows I'm worth more than many sparrows. A daughter who knows he watches me with love.[7]

☐ It Is Finished: Tender, Loving Care

Flip back to the pages with the list of carefree activities that children engage in. Select a few to try this week (the sooner the better). You may feel silly, but that's okay. Skip, twirl, run through the sprinklers, jump in mud puddles, lick melty ice cream from a waffle cone, or color a picture and put it on the fridge. Do whatever helps you rediscover the joy of being a daughter.

1. What activities did you choose?

2. How did you feel before, during, and after each activity?

3. Take some time to listen to the Father's tender, loving heart toward you, His girl. Write down what He reveals.

A Hired-Help Mentality Assessment

Put a check by each statement that you find yourself thinking, believing, or acting on. Don't censor yourself! This is not a verdict but an opportunity to evaluate honestly where you are in relation to a hired-help mentality.

- ☐ I am worth what I can earn.
- ☐ I could lose what I have at any given moment.
- ☐ I am afraid there will not be enough to go around, so I look out for myself at all costs.
- ☐ I feel as if I am often left out or left behind.
- ☐ Typically, "Yes" = Loved and "No" = Unloved.
- ☐ I have a hard time trusting and receiving love.
- ☐ I keep a record of wrongs done and revisit it often.
- ☐ I assume the worst and often am suspicious of others' motives.
- ☐ When I fail, I am hard on myself for messing up and replay the event over and over.
- ☐ When I succeed, I have difficulty celebrating the achievement, quickly looking to what is next.
- ☐ Other people's success feels like a threat to my happiness.
- ☐ Others might not meet my needs as I want them to, so I often meet my own.
- ☐ My behavior (good or bad) will ensure that others take notice of me.
- ☐ I resent God's boundaries for me and sometimes rebel against them.

(continued on the next page)

Look back over your answers. Underline one statement that is not something you struggle with. Then circle one statement that you find yourself struggling with often, and think about a specific circumstance that has contributed to your believing this particular lie. Ask God to help you entrust this situation to His keeping as you move away from a hired-help mentality toward a beloved daughter's mentality. Also, consider what truth, event, or revelation has helped you break free from the underlined statement. Thank God for His help in exposing this lie and embracing the truth.

Take some time to talk to God about the statement you circled. Journal your thoughts, draw a picture, or go for a walk and listen to what He has to say to you.

PART II

Sitting

You don't have to earn
your keep or fight for a
seat. Your worth is set-
tled and your position
is secure.

4

How Much Is Required?

The Completed Work of the Cross

❧

His love for me doesn't rest on my performance
but on what He performed on the cross.

—Niki Hardy

A four-year-old girl with a pixie haircut swings on the red metal swing set in the backyard. Under the lemon trees and an overcast California sky, she pumps her little legs back and forth, higher and higher, gazing toward the clouds and singing this prayer to the heavens: "Come into my heart, Lord Jesus; come in today, come in to stay."[1] In her childlike way, she asks Jesus in.

The Lord has brought this backyard memory to mind on more than one occasion. It was simple yet significant. As I swung, I welcomed in the Savior. No scripted prayer, no jumping through hoops, no paying my way—just childlike faith, declaring need.

I asked Jesus in again a few more times, just to be sure: when I was eight at Awana and then again in college after a revival sermon left me shaking in my boots, questioning whether I was saved. Looking back, these additional "conversions" were based on flawed theology that it was up to me to remain in right standing with God. As if my sinful post-salvation behavior could worm me out of God's favor. As if righteousness was a cloak that could be stripped off because I had dirtied myself again. As if Jesus's complete sacrifice was weaker than my sin.

LIVING UP TO ONE'S NAME

I am fascinated by the meaning of names. In Bible times, God changed people's names to reflect defining moments in their lives. Abram became Abraham ("father of many nations"). Sarai became Sarah ("mother of nations"). Jacob became Israel (the name of God's chosen people and their nation).

My name means "pure." In secret, I acted opposite of what my name declared. From a young age, impurity was a close companion. My hunger for significance, affection, and belonging trumped wisdom. A nonrefundable admittance fee was paid to open doors that led to a hallway of cheap substitutes. I tried to grab love through compromise and accomplishments.

When I graduated from my small-town high school, I couldn't wait to go to college and start a new life with a clean slate. Although I had been a believer in Jesus since I was four years old, I got serious about my faith in my freshman year of college. I began to fully understand that the Christian life is about a relationship with Jesus—not just learning about Him but also loving Him and being loved by Him. My faith became my own as I distanced myself from the poor decisions I had made. I surrounded myself with Christians, went to Bible studies, and tried to walk the line.

I got married a year after graduating from college, and Adam sometimes asked me about "high school Katie." I had confessed my secret sins to him while we were dating, but he was curious to understand who I used to be. I tried to change the subject. I didn't want to remember, because I was no longer that person. I didn't like impure Katie. She wasn't happy. She was conflicted, straddling the fence between the wilderness and the Promised Land. She was lonely and looking for love in all the wrong places, so I rejected her and moved on to a different life, trying not to look back.

About seven years ago, God tenderly showed me how I had cut off parts of my heart that I knew were ugly. He whispered, "You hate 'high school Katie,' but I don't. I loved you then just as much as I do now."

I worked hard to make myself presentable to God by locking up years of my life that were marked by shame. But with His assurance of love, I saw the importance of treating old Katie with kindness. If the Savior of the world could love her, I certainly could be nicer to her.

There is a difference between turning from sin (which is a good idea!) and putting part of your heart behind bars (not a good idea).

God called me "pure" from the time I was reborn into His family, there on the swing—not because I was pure in and of myself but because He took on my impurities as His own on the cross. He removed my sin and gave me His righteousness. Yet I still tried to put a part of me in a permanent time-out for having been a naughty young woman.

Later on in college, I swung to the other extreme as I hung out in Arrogance Alley, criticizing others for not meeting my holier-than-thou standards. I pleaded with the Lord to heap on blessings and then judged others for not being spiritual enough. Legalism puffed me up as I strove to be holier—working to earn a higher degree of spirituality, with a minor in shoddy theology.

I struggled to believe that Jesus's forgiveness and acceptance were unconditional. I thought that good works were the avenue to stay in right standing with the Lord. So when my works weren't so good, I assumed that Jesus was disappointed and distant. When I felt as though I made the grade, spiritually speaking, pride followed me around, like an honor-roll sticker slapped on the bumper of my powder-blue Dodge Omni.

Of course Jesus wants what is best for us and desires us to follow in His steps and grow more like Him. However, He does not love us any more or any less based on our behavior. He is both loving and just, both approachable and holy, both personal and powerful. Yes, there is wrath for sin. Yes, a perfect sacrifice was required to satisfy God's righteous anger toward iniquity (lustful impurity and legalistic piety alike). Yes, there is eternal judgment for those who *choose* to reject the free and gracious gift of salvation. But once we have truly believed in Jesus as Savior and received Him as Lord, we don't have to worry about losing our places as His children.

THE COST TO BRING YOU HERE

It is almost closing time at an amusement park as my friend Jen's son and my son Isaiah sit together on a mock speedboat, having a grand time. The sun is shining overhead as my friend and I watch our long-awaited, fervently prayed-for adopted sons circling before us on the ride. Time seems to slow. I quietly say to Jen, "Wow, just think about all it took to get these boys to this moment."

Jen and I both live busy, full lives, trying to keep our heads above water as the demands of parenting dictate much of our days. Each of our boys has his own story to tell, but the way they ended up in our arms is nothing short of miraculous. They might not have made it if God hadn't intervened. There were heartache, sacrifice, and great cost from many sides, but God made a way as only He can. Sure, there were things both Jen and her husband and Adam and I had to do to bring our kids home: fingerprinting, fund-raising, endless paperwork, and walking in faith when hope was hidden. We battled doubts, faced fears, and climbed over roadblocks, but the outcomes were God's doing.

When Adam and I began the journey of adding to our family through adoption, I was so focused on the end goal that I didn't stop to really think through how our gain would cost someone else a great deal of loss. It caught me off guard that joy and sadness could be so intermingled and even experienced at the same time.

There is a quote from adoptive mom Jody Landers that perfectly articulates the complicated feelings of adoptive parents: "Children born to another woman call me 'Mom.' The magnitude of that tragedy and the depth of that privilege are not lost on me."[2]

There are times Isaiah gets upset and acts out and I wonder whether it's because of his temperament or age or whether it's an adoption-related issue. Sometimes I act out when I don't get my way and it's based on my tightly wound temperament and *not* acting my age. But sometimes it's an adoption issue. I forget that I belong to God, my identity is secure, and Someone has gone to great lengths to bring me home.

As Jen and I watch our boys, our hearts are filled with the weight of the moment and a deep sense of thankfulness. And I wonder whether God also looks at us, His grown girls, and quietly says, "Look at all I did to get you here."

Adopting us into God's family came at a tremendous cost to His Son. Jesus was bloodied and broken so I could have the opportunity to be called "daughter." The magnitude of *that* tragedy and the depth of the privilege are not lost on me.

THE REQUIREMENT OF SURRENDER

It's humbling to recognize the excruciating sacrifice that was required of Jesus to redeem us. But once we admit our need for Him to save us from our sins and believe in what He has done on the cross, now what? What is required of us as Christ followers, in light of these truths? What are we doers to do?

Following God's lead is built on the foundation of surrendering control to Him and trusting that He knows best. This can be a challenge for get-it-done gals. Before I understood the heart of God toward me, I assumed that surrendering to Him (in small or major ways) would require a life of misery and living in a hut in a faraway country.

In her book *Control Girl,* author Shannon Popkin addressed this idea of surrender regarding a woman who *was* called to live in a tent (almost like a hut) in a country that was not her own (see Genesis 12): "When we picture surrendering to God, I think we sometimes picture a dreary, uphill climb. And many times it is. But our mental image of surrendering to God should also include a picture of Sarah holding Isaac on her lap, for it was surrender that brought this 'Laughter' to life."[3]

While God sometimes asks us to do hard things, those things are never wasted and serve a purpose far greater than we can imagine. There is a lightness that is birthed in our spirits when we realize that no matter what happens, we are delighted in, are held by, and belong to a good Father. We might not understand His ways—in fact, we might roll our eyes or stomp our feet as we face trials or restrictions—but I believe we will one day (whether down the road or in eternity) look back and see how God was always motivated by love for us.

THE MARCH OF PRODUCTIVITY

So where do works come in? Let's get to the nitty-gritty and roll out the to-do list so we can tackle it!

It's difficult to meet and exceed expectations if we don't know what they are or if they are too open ended. After people accept Jesus as Savior, they are often told to start reading their Bibles and praying. While these are great tools for growth, I think many of us confuse these and other spiritual disciplines with have-tos when it comes to our faith walks.

Let me first admit the trouble I have with the word *discipline*. That makes it sound as if I must spank myself into submitting to a life of drudgery as a Christ follower and always make sure my uniform is ironed (I don't iron). May I suggest "spiritual frosting" as a more appetizing option? Or a "spiritual smoothie" (with no GMOs, if that's your jam)? It's easier to swallow the treats of prayer, fasting, and Bible study when we view them as enjoyable opportunities to spend time with the One we adore, not as choke collars to keep us in line. When you get a taste of pure and unadulterated grace, you naturally (or supernaturally) gain an appetite for what grows your faith muscles. Your attitude toward the disciplines becomes healthier when you realize they are no longer the recipe for favor.

Often we think that spiritual disciplines, exemplary behavior, and good works pave the way to right standing with God. Modern-day believers often behave like the Levitical priests, who were required to follow a long list of procedures for sin removal. But on this side of the Cross, spiritual expectations have changed and we are freed from the need to wear ourselves out continually to be in right standing with God.

Abraham was, humanly speaking, the founder of our Jewish nation. What did he discover about being made right with God? If his good deeds had made him acceptable to God, he would have had something to boast about. But that was not God's way. For the Scriptures tell us, "Abraham believed God, and God counted him as righteous because of his faith."

When people work, their wages are not a gift, but something they have earned. But people are counted as righteous, not because of their work, but because of their faith in God who forgives sinners. (Romans 4:1–5, NLT)

Well-meaning Christians are living in self-imposed bondage, as I did for years. Many are bound by guilt that has already been pardoned, chained to service as a means to the favor they already have, or trying to keep the Law to obtain righteousness. Like that of the Pharisees, our thinking is short-sighted when we depend on our works to win us prominence.

Does following Christ cost us something? Of course.

Should our lives look different because of Christ's work in us? Definitely.

Should we obey the Lord? Yes!

But I'm afraid we sometimes confuse productivity with value and equate soul worth with intellectual, physical, and spiritual output.

I have a friend, Rachel, who has a chronic illness and cannot do all she wants to do. Her body requires nineteen to twenty hours of resting in bed to accomplish four or five hours' worth of light activity. There are times Rachel places unrealistic expectations on herself. She sometimes tries to do more than her body can physically handle and then is unable to complete the desired task. Her self-made to-do list places a burden on her that is often too heavy to bear. Rachel admits that sometimes her pride, her self-sufficiency, or simply forgetting how limited she is in strength and energy are reasons she tries to do more than she is able. When this happens, she reminds herself to go back to Scripture and see what God requires of her. She says, "He doesn't require that I complete my self-made to-do list. He doesn't ask me to use more energy than He has given me. He doesn't require me to keep my house perfectly clean. He requires that I love Him and serve Him with the strength He provides, not the strength I wish I had."[4]

Sometimes we can't "do" as we used to, can't give as much as we once could, or are unable to serve as others can because of commitments or limitations. Does this mean we are less loved, less worthy, less Christian? Of course not.

Our worth is solely dependent on the One in whose image we are made. That worth was cemented into our cells way before we could lift a finger or create to-do lists.

As I mentioned earlier, my brother has Down syndrome. His value, like yours and mine, is directly related to the fact that he is created in God's image. Brian is not "less than" because his productivity and functionality differ from mine. He has value because he exists. He doesn't have to prove his worthiness through good deeds, test scores, or gold medals (although he has loads of those from winning boccie-ball matches at the Special Olympics).

Brian doesn't have to work harder to be deemed enough. So why does his big sis struggle to apply to herself what she believes is true about him? I feel handicapped in my ability to change.

Finally, the other day, I said, "Okay, God, I can't make these changes on my own. I do what I don't want to do, but I can't seem to find my way out of this unhealthy cycle of striving. Would You please help me?"

It seemed that Jesus responded with a knowing smile and something like this: *Well, My child, it's about time you acknowledged that you can't do this without My help. Now we can make real progress.*[5]

Why do I wait to send up an SOS until I'm at the end of my rope? Why don't I go to Jesus first and admit my need? When you're used to operating under the perception that you can handle it, manage it, and produce it through your own strength and intellect, it's easy to forget your desperate need for the Savior.

The belief that productivity equals value is like kryptonite for modern Marthas. We are wired to work—which is a good thing—yet our greatest strengths can morph into our biggest weaknesses if left unchecked.

Ingrained into my American brain is this idea of entitlement: if I do A,

B, and C, then I will get X, Y, and Z. But God's economy does not work like that. Sure, there are blessings for obedience and consequences for disobedience. But the incredible gift of His grace is not extended to me because I've done enough good to gain it. It's more as if I flunked the test but Jesus decided to take my bad mark as His score even though He had a perfect GPA. Not only that, but He then took and passed the test on my behalf and gave me the A+ that He earned.

It used to drive me crazy when someone could get more than 100 percent on a test or project in high school through extra-credit options. But from a spiritual standpoint, extra credit doesn't pan out. You can't improve on what has already met the standard of perfection. Jesus provided all that was needed for our salvation; we cannot add to it. He completed the work. It is finished. *El fin*. The end.

This finality of salvation goes against my internal drive to do more.

Before I realize it, I have too many tabs open on the computer, too many things I am trying to accomplish at once. But all these tabs and things bog down my productivity.

Jesus sure did many things! Yet He didn't do all those things at once, and He didn't go beyond and do extra things that weren't required of Him. He didn't let people pleasing or a proving mentality derail Him from His mission of carrying out His Father's business.

As we look at the life of Jesus, we realize that He did nothing apart from the leading of the Father. He was so fully assured of His Father's wisdom and goodness that He did not stray from willingly surrendering to His lead. Jesus was a faithful steward of what was entrusted to Him and relied on God's strength to help Him get those things done.

Productivity does not equal worthiness. Busyness does not equal holiness. Spiritual activity doesn't earn us an A. We are worthy only because Christ is worthy. We are holy only because Christ is holy.

In Christ we have seats for our souls, even when we are on the go. We don't lose our seats when we aren't engaging in religious activities. What's true of us doesn't change with the gain or loss of abilities. What defines us as Christ's daughters follows us through activity and inactivity. We don't lose our position because of changing seasons, shifting hormones, or adverse situations.

We serve with the strength He gives as we follow the lead of the Spirit. We no longer march to the beat of imperious expectations; we hum the melody of grace and sway to the rhythm of peace. We rest within, knowing that our works are not the motivation for His love, nor are our mistakes cause for His love to be withheld. We don't make light of what was required for our freedom. Through Him, in Him, and with Him, we have everything that's required for worthiness and holiness.

Often on my Instagram feed, I see beautiful images of picture-perfect quiet times from godly women I esteem. A candle is lit or morning light is streaming in the window, and a steamy beverage and a flower in bloom frame an opened Bible and journal. I am not mocking the act of spending time with God; in fact, I recommend it. However, for too long I lived with guilt that if I didn't have an hour of intense study or completely silent communion with my Lord, I was a second-class Christian. I felt off if I didn't spend a certain amount of quality time with Jesus each day.

But when we understand the goodness of our heavenly Father, we trust Him more. "The practice of acknowledging God and living for Him rather than struggling to be known for our own accomplishments frees us from the need to jump from the highest platform or swim the deepest sea for the world's approval, and it carries the promise of enjoying His sweet presence— whether or not we've had a quiet time that morning!"[6]

We begin to understand that God's Word is full of wisdom to help us navigate life. And the invitation to follow Him is not a drag but a gift that grows our relationship with Him, strengthening our resolve and giving us front-row seats to witness majesty and miracles. When we understand how much we are loved and that we don't have to become someone else to keep that love, we begin to relax in His presence. His guidance is more readily received when we understand the heart behind it. How many times have we brushed off our parents' advice or rolled our eyes, only to realize later how right they were and that it was love for us that motivated them?

As one Twitter user said, "The degree to which your children trust you is the degree to which they will let you love them and influence them."[7] We learn to trust our heavenly Father's voice when we are assured of His love. As He instructs us to read the Word, as He prompts us to call out in prayer, as He leads us to surrender, we begin to see that these disciplines aren't to ruin our fun but to grow us in ways that are good for us.

A TALE OF TWO PARTIES

When I was in middle school, I was asked to assist with a large birthday party for an elementary-aged child. The party seemed to last all day. I worked as diligently as I could, doing what was requested and trying to prove I was worthy of the job I had been given. At the end of the day, I was worn out from putting my best foot forward and trying to match the enthusiasm and energy of the young partygoers. Payment had not been discussed prior to the event, so I labored hard, hoping to earn a hefty wage. I recall a twenty-dollar bill crossing my palm. It was probably more than fair for the early nineties, yet I had my sights set higher, hoping for double that amount. I expected a large return on my time and tireless contribution to the festivities but ended up disappointed.

Fast-forward to a party that took place several years ago. My sisters and I were asked to assist with a seventieth-birthday celebration. We gladly agreed. We mingled with guests, made them feel welcome, sang in three-part harmony, and wrote and performed a poem for the birthday boy. It was a fun, full night. No payment was expected; it was a privilege to be part of honoring the seventy-year-old. The reason for this was based not solely on the age of the individual but on our relationship to him. It was a celebration for our dad. My mom asked us to help her pull off a surprise gathering, and we were happy to do so. We are daughters of a kind and caring father, and being family was reward enough. We were willing to give of ourselves to bring joy to our dad's heart.

At the child's party, I was the hired help. At my dad's party, I was a beloved daughter. I worked hard at both events, but my motivation for doing so varied drastically, based on my relationship with the guest of honor. At the first party, I was driven by what I could prove and earn; at the second, by what I could sacrifice and offer.

Through a skewed view of what is required to be accepted, I relate to God as I did to the father of the birthday boy at the first party: proving and earning my way to reward, afraid of His disappointment (or even anger) if I don't do what is expected.

The hired-help mentality breeds insecurity. It robs us of peace. It views favor as something to be gained through good works. There is nothing wrong with doing good, but let's ask ourselves why we are doing it. Is it to express gratitude to God, or is it because we are afraid we will fall out of His good graces if we fail? Is it to help others because we love God and love them, or is it to make sure we are seen, praised, and deemed worthy? Is it for the good of others or an effort to be good enough?

The bad news is, we definitely are *not* good enough apart from Christ. The good news is, because of Christ, we don't have to be good enough in and of ourselves. Perfection is required, but we cannot achieve it. No amount of noble intentions, dazzling talent, or backbreaking labor on our parts can meet the requirement. So God sent Christ to meet it for us.

Understanding who our Father is, how much we've been given, and how adored we are in light of the Cross is a really big deal. It changes one's perspective on life, those around us, and the woman in the mirror. It's the difference between a life of grasping and being grounded. This grace thing is an invitation not to a life of compromise but one that stands on the promises of God with confidence. Through it, we transition from the slave mentality of earning our keep to a daughter's reality of enjoying what's ours.

Modern Martha Jan Greenwood

[Spiritual] orphans work hard for acceptance. Often those who struggle with this mind-set are achievers. They learn early that the uncomfortable sensation of feeling abandoned or alone can be calmed by doing—and by the positive feedback given to great doers. This leads to a vicious cycle that often takes a type of breaking in order to overcome. I have found that being sick has made me weak. I literally can't "do" as I used to. When you can no longer perform to the standard you have set—or the standard others have become quite comfortable with—you can really have a fearful identity crisis. If I don't "do," then I'm not sure "who" I am. A slave is driven to work—they must—even unto death. But a daughter works in response to love. She belongs to the Father. Therefore, she has a place in His presence at all times. Out of a sense of safety and belonging, her "do" will spring forth, right in alignment with her gifts and destiny. It becomes natural rather than forced. It has anointing rather than sweat. Who we are and who we belong to are such foundational issues that must be settled for all of us.[8]

☐ It Is Finished: The ABCs of Eternal Acceptance

Utilize this handy acrostic exercise to remember the three requirements necessary for right standing with God.

Admit: Admit that your sins have separated you from God and that you can never do enough to earn your salvation.

Believe: Believe that Jesus is God's Son and that He lived a perfect life, died for your sins on the cross, and rose again so you can be forgiven and freed.

Claim: Receive what Jesus has done for you by faith and claim your place as His daughter, restored to the Father through the only way possible: the blood of His Son.

5

Are You in a Swivel Chair or Comfy Recliner?

Grace with No Strings Attached

❧

If it's the right chair, it doesn't take too long to get comfortable in it.

—Robert De Niro

When I was a girl, I used to belt out show tunes and twirl in the living room. I adjusted the movable lamp atop our piano so that its light bounced off the ceiling, cascading from heaven. Decked in a black leotard, I sang my heart out, pretending I was on *Star Search* (the *American Idol* of the eighties). I performed with all my might to earn the applause of the couch audience, real and imagined.

Back in those days, I could spin and spin without it debilitating me. When I performed, I felt alive. I sang loud and spun fast, and it energized me. As I have gotten older, I still try to wow audiences with my performances, although I no longer wear a leotard (thank goodness!). The applause I crave now comes in the form of thumbs-ups, Likes, hearts, shares, and stats. I put on my Miss Dependability sash and pile on responsibilities. I strap on the weighty backpack as I head out for the day. I tie on an apron as I prepare for company. I do good works to gain worth. I try hard and work fast, but it electrocutes me. My efforts to be the best zap me of energy and burn up joy.

But I'm stubborn, so although I am tempted to give up at times, I keep going, trying to muster the strength and resolve to overcome my limitations. I advance like a robot, not a human.

Arriving at the desired goal, meeting the crowd's expectations, or being enough is like a steep climb where you never reach the top—kind of like the hike up the Sleeping Bear Dunes on the shores of Lake Michigan. You start off strong, and then after an endless incline, your calves are on fire and you're crawling on all fours, trying to make some sort of progress. You paw your way forward, determined to achieve what you set out to do. Then, as you finally reach what you think is the top, a mountain of sand, steeper than before, looms overhead. It appears to reach the heavens. The task seems impossible. Crying is a viable option.

I wander through the desert of self-effort on this faith journey, trying to reach the Promised Land. Determined to prove my worth, I fall short. My pilgrimage is parallel to my one and only gymnastic meet, where in sixth grade, while again wearing a leotard, I fell off the beam—five times. I was humiliated. My best wasn't good enough. But it wasn't for a lack of trying.

I still try to earn a high score, but I miss the mark. I flounder on my quest for perfection. And I am faced with a choice: I can cry about what feels impossible, or I can cry out to the One who can deliver me.

TURNING AND RETURNING

For four hundred years, the Hebrews lived as slaves in Egypt under the harsh rule of Pharaoh, but God heard the cries of His people and delivered them through Moses. God demonstrated signs and wonders in the form of ten plagues to make clear that He was Lord (see Exodus 7:5). God instituted the first Passover before the tenth plague fell on the people. The Hebrews were instructed to smear the blood of a perfect lamb on the tops and sides of the doorframes of their homes. Because of the blood, the angel of death passed over them. God's people were spared, but all the Egyptian firstborns died, including Pharaoh's son. The final plague proved too much for Pharaoh, so he finally allowed the Hebrews to go. In fact, he demanded it.

Not only did God bring the Hebrews out of bondage in Egypt, but He also divided the Red Sea for them and guided them with a cloud by day and with light from fire at night. He split rocks in the wilderness and gave His people water as abundant as the seas. But the Israelites continued to sin against Him, rebelling in the wilderness and grieving Him in the wasteland. They did not believe in God or trust in His deliverance. Despite His praiseworthy deeds, His power, and all the wonders He had performed, they kept sinning and did not believe. Again and again, they put God to the test and did not remember what He had done (see Psalm 78:13–18).

It was as if they were in a swivel chair. When God did what they wanted, they turned toward Him. Then they forgot and did their own thing, turning away from Him. Then God gave them a consequence and they turned back to Him. Because of their disobedience and unbelief, the Hebrews wandered in the desert for forty years.[1]

Whenever God slew them, they would seek him;
    they eagerly turned to him again.
They remembered that God was their Rock,
    that God Most High was their Redeemer.
But then they would flatter him with their mouths,
    lying to him with their tongues;

their hearts were not loyal to him,

they were not faithful to his covenant.

Yet he was merciful;

he forgave their iniquities

and did not destroy them.

Time after time he restrained his anger

and did not stir up his full wrath.

He remembered that they were but flesh,

a passing breeze that does not return. (verses 34–39, NIV)

God slew, and then they spun back around, returning to Him. It was a dizzying display of swiveling, to say the least.

The Israelites, newly out of slavery, questioned God's ability to be enough for them: "Can God really spread a table in the wilderness? True, he struck the rock, and water gushed out, streams flowed abundantly, but can he also give us bread? Can he supply meat for his people?" (verses 19–20, NIV).

What they were really asking was "Can He be trusted to care for us?"

In spite of their disobedience, questions, and swiveling, God did not abandon His plan for their total deliverance.

More than a thousand years after the first Passover in Egypt, Jesus gathered His disciples in an upper room in Jerusalem. He broke bread, poured wine, and pointed to His coming death. The perfect Lamb, God's beloved Son, was about to be sacrificed to deliver His people from the bondage of sin. A second exodus was about to transpire.

Through Christ, a communion table with broken body and spilled blood was spread in the midst of spiritual wilderness. Our sin separated us from God, but instead of leaving us to die in the wasteland of it, He sent Jesus to reconcile our wandering hearts to Him. God gave the Bread of heaven to be ravaged for our sin. God allowed the Rock of Ages to be struck, blood gush-ing out, that we might be delivered from slavery. He supplied the spotless Lamb for sacrifice.

Through the shed blood of Christ, the angel of death passes over the doorposts of all who choose to believe in Him. The manna, the water, the bread, the blood are provided through Jesus, for the Israelites and for the Gentiles, as a complete sacrifice for atonement. For you and me.

We have been given everything we need to be cleansed. We don't have to be perfect, we don't have to live spotless lives, because Jesus always is and already did. Our works will never be enough to pay our way to heaven. Our efforts will never fulfill what the Law requires. The Law demands perfection. It points us to our need for the Passover Lamb. And Jesus came and fulfilled what we could not.

Jesus gave all that we might gain all. His death on the cross made a way for us to go from slavery to freedom. We walk through the Red Sea of His blood and we are new—a people set apart for Him. We dance; we sing; we twirl with joy. We reflect the Light, saturating the darkness with hope. We applaud the One who performed flawlessly.

Since we have confidence to enter the holy places by the blood of Jesus, by the new and living way that he opened for us through the curtain, that is, through his flesh, and since we have a great priest over the house of God, let us draw near with a true heart in full assurance of faith, with our hearts sprinkled clean from an evil conscience and our bodies washed with pure water. Let us hold fast the confession of our hope without wavering, for he who promised is faithful. (Hebrews 10:19–23)

Too often I place my confidence in what I can offer—what I can do to maintain a clear conscience. I know that Christ has washed me white as snow, yet I labor to keep myself pure by dosing regularly with the bleach of good works. It is a tiring cycle of stain fighting as I try to reclean what is already spotless. In the middle of my misguided efforts to keep myself in good standing, Jesus invites me to take a seat.

DUSTY REVELATION

Our family calendar was bursting at the seams. Work responsibilities, hosting company, and ministry opportunities packed our schedule to the brim. We hoped for a break, but that wasn't the story God penned during this season. Oh, and did I mention that our fifth child was born too? Her name is Larkin, and we often shorten it to Lark, which means "spiritual freedom." God used this pregnancy to bring me back to Him and my family in many ways, but I had no idea the kind of spiritual freedom He would unleash soon after her arrival.

About three months after Lark was born, my friend Jami and I were in the midst of one of our rapid-fire phone conversations, where we pour out ideas, share enthusiasm for creative projects, and talk a mile a minute. From the heart of Texas, Jami declared that God was changing everything for her. She was at the tail end of writing her book, *Stolen Jesus,* when God gave her a fresh revelation of Jesus's completed work on the cross and what that meant for daily life. She was undone by the realization that there was nothing she needed to do to earn God's favor. She already had it—not because of her works but because of His. She didn't have to run a marathon, pray the rosary, or save a whale to please God. She couldn't help but share the good news. As she talked, I was skeptical. This grace without condition, "Jesus plus nothing"[2] talk, sounded too good to be true for a wound-up woman like me. But I listened closely and listened well, because I could not deny the freedom that I heard in my friend's voice.

For as long as I can remember, I have lived as though it is up to me to keep God and everyone else pleased. As I listened to Jami explain what God was revealing about grace, I started to come to, as if from a groggy sleep. My senses were heightened as this scene unfolded in my mind's eye:

I am in my living room, standing on the orange shag carpeting of our seventies A-frame home. Near the couch, I frantically pick up toys and stray clothing, scrambling to make my home presentable for company. I dust anxiously and hurry to declutter before the honored guest arrives. Then suddenly I realize there is a well-worn plaid recliner in the middle of the living room and Jesus is on it, relaxing—reading the newspaper, of all things. There I am, busily getting ready while He hangs out as if He lives here.

I turn toward Jesus. He puts the paper down.

He smiles.

Katie, you can stop getting ready for Me to come over. I'm already here. I live here, remember?

How did I forget that Jesus lives here, in the home of my heart? That's what they teach in Sunday school, but my legalistic wanderings have led me away from this beautiful reality.

You are trying to clean up your home, and your heart, to make yourself presentable. But I've presented Myself flawless. I've been found blameless. The work of salvation is finished. My love for you has been proved. You don't have to earn what is given to you as a gift.

Metaphorically, Jesus is reclining, right in the center of my home—my heart—in the dusty living room, on the orange shag. There, beneath the peaked ceiling, He sits. He is not in a hurry. He is at ease—at home.

I am sitting down, so you can too. Here, come relax with Me.

I usually make things complicated, but this sounds—dare I say it?—simple. To sit down, spiritually speaking, sounds like a vacation (the all-inclusive kind).

"But what about works, Jesus? Those are important too. Faith without works is dead, right?"

My daughter, there will be time for that, but your works aren't a means to obtain My salvation; they are a response to being saved. Doing good deeds is not a way to earn My love, but it is a response to being loved by Me.

Katie, Katie, you are worried and bothered by all that needs to be done, yet the one thing, number one on the list, the most important thing, has already been done. Yes, I know you are a doer like my dear Martha. I made you that way on purpose. But your serving, your doing, should be a response of gratitude, not a means to gain what I've already freely given to you.

Maybe I have it all backward. I have been busy cleaning the outside of the cup while the inside cracks from all the pressure I put on it (see Matthew 23:25–26). Yet there in my imperfections, in my home, I am put back together—already whole, already clean— because Jesus took the cup of God's wrath for my sin. And because I have believed in Jesus and received Him as Savior, God is not mad or disappointed in me—or in you.

Your sins are not temporarily covered; they are permanently removed, as far as the east is from the west. You have been trying to clean up, but you are already clean. You have been trying to make yourself spotless, but you already are, because I AM. Spotless. Blame- less. Clean. The Passover Lamb slain so that you can be spared. My blood canceled the debt you owed.

You are free from measuring up, because I overturned the scales of sin and shame. When you fall short or fall down, My robe of righteousness remains on you like a coat of many colors, boldly reflecting My unwavering delight in you.

Years of striving screech to a halt as this living-room revelation brings grace into focus. Joy courses through my body as my soul takes its foot off the accelerator and sits down. I can breathe deeply. I can think clearly. Amazed at the simplicity yet depth of this epiphany of grace, I am like a child on Christmas morning. Wonder fills my weary frame. Spiritual liberty is born (cue the fireworks). After decades of toil, I am released. After forty years of bondage, I am set free; I'm no longer a slave. After years of wandering, I come home, because I remember that He is at home, in me: "Christ will make his home in your hearts as you trust in him. Your roots will grow down into God's love and keep you strong" (Ephesians 3:17, NLT).

PERFECT GIFT

Months after this encounter, a mug of elderberry tea is to my left, and an empty Styrofoam container from a Korean takeout sits in a plastic bag to my right. My daughter Brooke is attending an ornament-making party at a local pottery shop. While I wait to pick her up, I sit down to write at a church called Grace. I look out the window at a life-sized nativity, at the intersection of Preston and Mission in our small Michigan town. Vintage statuettes are strategically placed on a bed of hay. They have chipped paint here and there, which seems rather fitting. From my vantage point, I see the top of baby Jesus's head. Kneeling beside him is Mother Mary. Her hand is open and raised slightly, in worship of the Promised One.

Mary kneels by the feet of baby Jesus, maybe in a similar position to that of another Mary (Martha's sister) about three decades later. The value of this Gift, laid before Mother Mary and sitting in the home of the other Mary, seems to have been understood by both women as their posture communicates receptivity to His company.

Here, from my seated position, straining intersects the sacred—at the corner of Grace, on Mission. Saturday shoppers hurry past as calm Christmas music floats through the air. I'm hushed as I take in the sharp contrasts of hustle and holy, occupying shared space. I smile as my thoughts turn back to a Christmas memory from years gone by.

The majority of my childhood was spent in the eighties, when stonewashed jeans, tall bangs (held in place by an obscene amount of aerosol hair spray), and Madonna were all the rage. A few years before I was introduced to Madonna's music on MTV, Cabbage Patch Kids sprouted onto the scene.

In case you aren't familiar with these coveted icons, I'll refer to a late-night text exchange between my sisters to explain:

MARY: What exactly is a Cabbage Patch Kid?
LAURA: I have no idea. They spring from cabbages, but I think they
    are babies. With autographs on their buns?
MARY: And they all need to be adopted? Very confusing narrative.

People lost their minds over these dolls. Cabbage Patch Kids took the top spot on wish lists, and parents were willing to throw punches to get their little darlings some of them.

One Christmas morning, my aunt Florie called from Seattle so she could hear our reactions as we opened our gifts from her. She is a most thoughtful and generous gift giver, and my siblings and I couldn't wait to discover what was inside the meticulously wrapped packages.

Wide eyed, we tore open the boxes, scrambling to discover their contents. Could they be what we were secretly hoping for?

Yesss! Cabbage Patch Kids! We screamed with glee, jumped up and down, grinned from ear to ear, and thanked her profusely. My aunt must have enjoyed the blissful racket of our astonishment as we delighted in her gifts. She definitely earned "Aunt of the Year" that Christmas morning.

I felt like the luckiest kid on the block. This treasured doll was mine! And her name was Madeline. It almost seemed too good to be true. I felt deeply loved to receive such a gift. It was just right. It was a big deal!

How strange would it have been if, after receiving this gift, I had told my aunt that I would come and do her dishes, shovel her driveway, or give her all the money in my piggy bank? Or what if I had made a well-meaning promise to always be a good girl so that I'd somehow be worthy of the lavish gift she purchased for me? She wouldn't have heard of it. She probably would have said, "Your receiving my gift with gratitude is all I want in return. Enjoy it! You don't have to work for what I chose to give you." If I had tried to pay her back, whether in chores or cash, it would have been insulting. She did something special for us, and it wasn't because we were perfect children. It was because she loved us; we were family.

So why have I tried to earn what Christ has freely given? My actions communicate that chores, cash, and promises of good behavior are needed to be a worthy recipient of Jesus's lavish gift of salvation. But that's not how it works, because grace is a gift to be received, not a prize to be earned. And Jesus has already won the title "Savior of the Ages." He's the best gift giver of all time. We don't have to work to repay Him. He has already paid our debt. We receive His gift with gratitude and we enjoy it. We acknowledge the cost of grace and we feel like the luckiest in the world. A proper response to this undeserved gift might be shrieking with glee, jumping up and down, grinning from ear to ear, and thanking the Giver profusely.

THE RECLINER OF RECEPTIVITY

I have a receptivity deficiency. One time I told my husband, "I bet you feel like you can never do enough to make me feel loved. I know you love me, but my heart has a hard time receiving that love." And I know that Jesus loves me, but I have difficulty accepting it. The hired-help mentality shortchanges my capacity to receive and give love without condition. It stunts my ability to receive and extend grace with no strings attached. It's like a boss generously sending his employees on an all-expenses-paid trip to a destination of their choosing—I appreciate the offer but decide to earn my way instead of enjoying what has already been graciously provided. My way is paid in full, yet I try to pay again instead of accepting what has already been settled on my account.

Modern Marthas thrive on doing but struggle with receiving. They feel guilty and try to compensate the giver. Their doer hearts help many but can also work against their ability to be helped. And sometimes they silence the Helper, who resides within as they push forward, trying to meet a requirement that has already been satisfied.

When I read life's instruction manual, the Bible, it sometimes bellows like a prosecutor, exposing my unfit places and demanding I improve, or else. Sometimes it's like when I step on the scale and the number staring back taunts me so I spiral into a disgruntled state or am determined to work harder than ever. But after the dusty-living-room revelation of His grace, I hear a tender voice unwrapping love page by page, verse by verse, line by line. The Father comes into focus. I hear His kind instruction as I witness His commitment to my well-being—His unwavering fierceness on behalf of His children, like a ferocious lion protecting cubs.

I wake up, as if from a daze. I read Scripture with wide eyes as the good news erupts in an unabashed display of light. I catch a glimpse of iridescent grace, and everything looks shiny and new. Like a color-blind person seeing the vividness of autumn leaves for the first time, I gasp.

How did I miss this beauty? What have I been doing all this time? Why on earth did I allow myself to be lulled to sleep spiritually by swallowing lies such as these shown below?

- Performance determines worth.
- Good works lead to right standing with God.
- God's pleasure is directly correlated to what I do or don't do.

My tendency is to whip myself back into shape or beat myself up when I get off track, but the Father draws me close—not for chastisement but to demonstrate compassion. His gentle redirection guides me back to truth. His kindness leads to repentance (see Romans 2:4). He does not require us to earn what He has given; He wants us to just receive it, receive Him. This reality is not a license to abuse grace but an opportunity to adore the Grace Giver.

Our past is forgiven, our present is promising, and our future is secure. Our souls can rest in Christ's sufficiency (not swiveling!). Our hearts can relax in the arms of the One who holds us. This spiritual rest and heart settling demonstrate our belief in and receptivity to the greatest Doer of all time.

Jesus is sitting at home in our hearts—reclining in the living room, so to speak.

And it's such good news.

Modern Martha Jennifer Dukes Lee

I often pull an empty chair into my office when I'm working. And then I invite Jesus to sit there. I'm a very visual person, and this is a visual reminder to me that I am not working alone. The chair reminds me that He is "in this" with me ... because He called me to it! He does not abandon my work. And He doesn't meet me ONLY in my quiet time. He is with me as I manage work tasks and household responsibilities.

During the day, when I'm working in my office, I often pause, face the chair, and have an internal conversation with Jesus about what I'm feeling, what I'm carrying, what I need to lay down, what annoys me, what burdens me ... but also what makes me happy, what brings me delight, and how I'm so grateful that I don't do any of this alone.

So then ... even as I work, I feel a sense of internal peace and rest.[3]

☐ It Is Finished: Grace in the Desert

Read Jeremiah 31:2–6 in both the Message and the Voice versions. Take a few moments to write your response to this good news here.

6

Possessing What's Already Yours

Enjoying Your Spiritual Inheritance

❧

The father said to him, "Son, you are always with
me, and all that is mine is yours."

—Luke 15:31, AMP

$\mathcal{I}$n the shocking article "My Family's Slave," journalist Alex Tizon confesses that his parents owned a modern-day slave. They called her
Lola; they never paid her. She was ill treated and abused for decades. After
Alex's mother died, Lola went to live with Alex and his family. She was no
longer a slave, but because she had lived a lifetime as one, she had difficulty
making the shift to freedom in his home. Alex described it like this:

> It irritated me to catch her eating meals standing in the kitchen, or
> see her tense up and start cleaning when I walked into the room. One
> day, after several months, I sat her down.
>
> "I'm not Dad. You're not a slave here," I said, and went through a
> long list of slavelike things she'd been doing. When I realized she was
> startled, I took a deep breath and cupped her face, that elfin face now

looking at me searchingly. I kissed her forehead. "This is *your* house now," I said. "You're not here to serve us. You can relax, okay?"

"Okay," she said. And went back to cleaning.

She didn't know any other way to be. I realized I had to take my own advice and relax. If she wanted to make dinner, let her. Thank her and do the dishes. I had to remind myself constantly: *Let her be.*

One night I came home to find her sitting on the couch doing a word puzzle, her feet up, the TV on. Next to her, a cup of tea. She glanced at me, smiled sheepishly with those perfect white dentures, and went back to the puzzle. *Progress,* I thought.[1]

It's tempting to keep living like the hired help—not because that way of life is easy or fulfilling but because it's what we have known. We revert to slave-like tendencies and thought patterns because they're familiar; we know the way. We chase our tails as we wear paths (and ourselves) into the ground. We keep trying to do it all, yet we never can, nor do we have to.

Our spiritual freedom is dependent on another's faithfulness. And God's faithfulness does not and cannot fail. Our part in the deal is to believe and receive His perfection for our imperfection and live in light of that good news. Our redeemed role is to enjoy what is ours and learn to walk out the freedom we already possess. It sounds simple, but it's a big challenge for those who have lived tethered to the law of self-effort and chained to the principle of behavior modification. After years of relying on ourselves, it feels unsettling to trust another to care for us.

NAVIGATING ABUNDANCE

Two of my friend's children were adopted from a war-torn country in Africa. Survivors of trauma, they arrived with complicated needs and bloated bellies. Children who have not been given enough food in the past will often hoard it when they're brought into a home where there is plenty. They hide food under their beds, stuff it into their pockets, and ask for it incessantly. Their physical hunger mirrors their emotional appetite to be filled up with love. Even though the fridge and cupboards are full, they still have to be assured of what's true: "You will be taken care of. You are loved and I will give you what you need. There is enough here for you—more than enough." Over time, trust grows as their needs are continually met, and their brains can be reprogrammed to have healthier relationships with food and with loved ones.

Sometimes we possess a great deal, but having lived so long without realizing we have it, we don't tap into what is ours. Like a child who gorges herself even though she has access to an endless supply of food, or a slave who keeps serving even when she has been freed from earning her keep, we take time to navigate and embrace the new reality of being beloved daughters.

Recently, one of the big-box stores in our town remained open for business while undergoing major reconstruction and remodeling. Each time I bravely (or some might say *foolishly*) entered the store, I quickly became disoriented, as various sections were moved from week to week. Prior to this project, I knew what most of the aisles contained. But during the project, I felt lost and aimless, uncertain of where I was headed or what I even needed.

Leaving behind spiritual slavery—earning my keep and position through good works—is somewhat disorienting. Even though spiritual freedom is meant to be a wide-open field, inviting me to run, dance, or lie down, it resembles the shopping experience. I'm not sure where to turn first. The old staples of striving, image management, and overdoing it are no longer required, so what's a doer to do? I haven't walked this way before, and I'm not sure whether I'm headed in the right direction. Even though the new setup is better, it's hard to get used to it, as I realize my know-how is no longer my go-to. I'm still a doer through and through, but how I walk is adjusted as I learn a new way of living. Sometimes I bump into things and look clumsy, but I'm making progress. Occasionally, I relapse and revisit the well-worn pathways of the hired-help mentality, yet these setbacks don't change the freedom that is mine.

Maybe our greatest "doing" is believing what has already been done. Maybe our biggest accomplishment is learning to lean into Christ's sufficiency. Maybe our most noble assignment is to operate in what is already true and live out the benefits of daughtership instead of the bonds of slavery.

I can hear the hecklers now: "Wait a minute, Ms. Katie. There are lots of verses in the Bible about being a slave of Christ." Oh, my dear, I know. But might I suggest that those like Paul, a bondslave of the Lord, knew the Master for who He is: an omnipotent Deity, not a tyrannical taskmaster? And a bondslave is one who willingly places himself back under the authority of the One who has freed him. You are compelled to choose to do that when your Master is kindhearted and generous, which is exceedingly true of our Lord.

The biggest differences between a hired-help mentality and a beloved daughter's mentality are these:

- One is grounded in fear; the other is rooted in faith.
- One boasts of self-dependence; the other confesses Savior dependence.
- One is based on grasping; the other is founded on receptivity.
- One is fueled by unrest; the other is powered by soul rest.

It seems like a no-brainer to choose a beloved daughter's reality over a hired-help mentality. But often our mind-sets have stubborn roots. It feels safer when it's all up to us instead of when we have to depend on another.

As it was for the slave Lola, it's a natural tendency to rely on what you have known for so long. As you learn to utilize what you already possess, don't boss yourself around or stick yourself in the corner as you find your footing. Be patient with yourself. Give yourself space and grace as you learn to think and act differently.

I wonder whether the Israelites struggled to find their footing as they wandered in the desert. The predictable yet grueling monotony of brick-making and oppressive toil was not their reality anymore. Even though it was a relief to be released from slavery, it was a strange feeling not knowing what to do exactly. Sure, they followed God via the cloud by day and the fire by night, but they weren't sure what they might encounter day to day or when the massive relocation project would end.

SURVEYING THE LAND

When my husband and I bought our first home, we looked at only one house: a hilltop Cape Cod that needed some TLC. We made an offer and it was accepted. One and done. But twelve years later, when it was time to buy another home, we had a different experience. Five months of active house hunting was met with five rejected offers. Just when we thought we'd found "the one," it slipped through our fingers. It was a roller coaster of emotions for our whole family. Eventually, a seventies A-frame with oodles of charm and four acres of parklike bliss caught our attention. As we walked the grounds, our hearts quickened. I wonder whether it was a little like how Caleb and Joshua felt as they surveyed the Promised Land, amazed at what they saw. We didn't find clusters of grapes, but we did find clusters of fragrant lilacs, a rushing creek, and an expanse of green lawn wrapping around a pond of still waters. We laughed. We teared up. We couldn't believe our eyes.

Our son Kale repeatedly stopped around the property to ask God to give us this house and land. At one point, he took a knee in the grass and prayed. At another point, he rounded us up as a family on the front patio and said, "I think we need to pray again."

We were told that another couple was coming back to look at the house again, so as soon as we left the property, we put in an offer. We were afraid we might get outbid, but later that evening our offer was accepted! And there was loud, shout-it-from-the-rooftops rejoicing when we heard the good news!

Plot twists and looming giants threatened our happy ending, but we held on. Sometimes possessing what is ours comes with a fight. Let me be clear: giants in the land doesn't mean that God won't be faithful to His promise, but battling against them is often required as we exercise faith and trust God to come through. Just because something doesn't come easily doesn't make it less true or less ours. However, it's important to differentiate between our role in the process and God's. Let's revisit our friends the Israelites to understand this more fully.

The Promised Land was given to the Hebrews by God, yet to occupy the land, they had to subdue it. In Deuteronomy 9:1–6, God told the Israelites that they were about to dispossess nations that were greater and stronger than they were, such as the giant-sized Anakites. God assured them that He would go ahead of them and destroy and subdue the people who were in the land He had promised them. But He required the Israelites to carefully follow His instructions and be active participants during this conquest. God promised He would give His people victory but said they needed to believe Him and act on that belief.

God also warned the Israelites not to take credit for the victory or base their success on their own righteousness. It is on account of God's faithfulness that His people possessed the land that He gave them and enjoyed its abundance. The credit belonged to God. His goodness to them was not based on their behavior; it was based on Him fulfilling His promise to them. Their works did not earn them this reward, but His grace gave them undeserved favor.

Modern Marthas are competent and capable women who put many hours in. There is nothing wrong with that; it is how we are wired. Our get-it-done attitude keeps bellies full, schedules managed, and deadlines met. Yet it's important to remember that our success has more to do with God's ability and faithfulness than ours. We cooperate with Him and nothing is impossible, yet in and of ourselves (apart from Him), we have no good thing. A dear Mary friend of mine, Lee, wisely reminded me of this when I was in the middle of writing. I relied on my ability to accomplish the God-sized task and tried to please Him in my own strength. Lee lovingly reminded me that the task of writing this book was dependent on His faithfulness, not my ability. She texted, "Katie can't, but God in Katie can." Her loving exhortation humbled me in the best kind of way. As I transferred the burden onto God's capable shoulders, I felt released to do my part and trust Him to do His.

LIVING OUT WHAT'S TRUE

England's Queen Elizabeth was born into a royal family. When her uncle abdicated, her father became king. Upon her father's passing, she became queen. She not only knew what was true about her position, but she also began living out that position through her words and actions. There has been a cost to her reign: being misunderstood, scrutinized, and criticized by many while facing difficult personal and professional decisions. The position is not easy, but she is committed to honoring the Crown and what it represents. She has walked out who she is in light of what she was born into.

Understanding that we are daughters is important, but living out the reality of what that means is crucial. Let's examine another royal to help us move from knowing what's true to acting on it. In a powerful sermon about King Solomon, a pastor explained that Solomon had been given the gift of wisdom by the Lord (see 1 Kings 3:9–12) but to exercise that gift, he had to believe he had received it and walk it out in faith. Soon after Solomon received the gift of wisdom, he was given the opportunity to use it.

Two women who were harlots came to the king, arguing over a baby. Both women claimed that the child was theirs, but Solomon, in his newfound wisdom, said he would cut the child in two. The child's actual mother insisted that the king give her baby to the other woman so that her son wouldn't be harmed. Because of this, Solomon knew that she was the rightful mother of the child.

In verse 28 we read, "When all Israel heard the king's decision, the people were in awe of the king, for they saw the wisdom God had given him for rendering justice" (NLT).

Like the slave Lola, Queen Elizabeth, and King Solomon, we possess what is ours when we live out what is true in light of our identity. We are no longer orphans but heirs, no longer slaves but royalty, no longer hired help but beloved daughters.

Sometimes it's tempting to take credit for what we have or to assume, wrongly, that our success is a direct result of our own doing. We may think, *I have this because I worked hard for it.* While there might be some truth to that, God is the one who gave you the ability to work. He is the one who wove your body together so that you could do the work. He gave you breath so you could be alive right now. It all depends on Him. We are active participants, but He supplies the victory.

We are doers, but it is by His doing that we can do in the first place. It's not because we are so great but because He is. We may face giants, hardship, and years of wandering as we journey in faith, yet none of that changes the good news of grace. It's ours. We have been given more than we realize. And now the time has come to possess what's been provided.

OWNERSHIP AND POSSESSION

Once we had signed all the papers for the purchase of our new A-frame home, it was ours by law. How strange would it have been if we'd never taken possession of it? What if we had just said, "Hey, see that house? It's ours. Isn't it fantastic?" But our friends would've scratched their heads, wondering why we had not moved in and gotten settled. It would've been even stranger if, instead of living in our new home, we had lived in a tent.

There is a difference between owning something and possessing it. Possessing is interacting with something in a way that depicts ownership. It's using what we have, not just admiring it from a distance. We have some wealthy friends who own many expensive things, yet their busy schedule rarely affords them time to enjoy what is theirs. I have done a similar thing from a spiritual standpoint. I know what is true legally: Jesus has purchased my salvation with His blood, He's justified me, and He wants to "buy [me] from the slave market of sin"[2] by adopting me into God's family. It's a done deal. Yet it's baffling that I often don't live out the benefits of what is now mine. It's like saying, "Hey, I'm a daughter of the King," but never tapping into the perks of that title, never settling into the position, always questioning whether it is true (even though *all* that was necessary has been accomplished to make it so).

Possessing what is ours is an important part of walking confidently as daughters. As we do so, let's give thanks to the One who establishes our position and secures our inheritance. May His abundant gifts draw us closer to Him and let us know how deeply loved we are. May we not become entitled brats who think our blessing is due us because we are so exceptional. May His mercy and kindness keep us humble as we realize that, thankfully, God does not give us what we deserve. May we enjoy the wonderful benefits of being

His, here on earth, as we look forward to the day when we will receive an all-access pass to the Promised Land:

> Lord, you alone are my portion and my cup;
>> you make my lot secure.
> The boundary lines have fallen for me in pleasant places;
>> surely I have a delightful inheritance. (Psalm 16:5–6, niv)

THE PRIZE PACKAGE

For years, I tried so hard to earn approval, when all I needed to do was enjoy what had been given to me. It's as if I felt hungry but had forgotten that I had just eaten Thanksgiving dinner:

> Appetites insatiable, stuffing and gorging
>> themselves left and right with people and things.
> But still they starved. Not even their children
>> were safe from their rapacious hunger. (Isaiah 9:20, msg)

I was starved for affection and hungry for love—malnourished even though I had the bounty of the King's table at my disposal. I hadn't really partaken of my Father's abundant supply of love; instead, I had made myself sick with quick fixes of sugary affirmations that never seemed to satisfy. On my quest to be filled, I had bypassed what was already available to me.

A timely letter from my friend Kaitlyn whispered a message my tired heart needed to hear:

> You are already a good mom, a good friend, and a good writer. You
> are already beloved, treasured, and cherished. What would happen if

you fully believed it? He is a God of the Already's and has declared you as such. Put on freedom today—it's already yours. Fix your eyes on what is good and true.[3]

Already. What a beautiful word. My striving soul stalled out as I took my foot off the gas and breathed in the present moment. I don't have to earn His love; I just need to receive it. I don't have to figure it all out. I lean in to His "already," and there I find "enough." I want my actions to communicate that Jesus is already enough for me. I don't want to act like the hired help when I'm already a beloved daughter. I don't want to just sing that His grace is enough; I want to live out the lyrics, that those in slavery might be free.

Bible teacher Carrie Gaul confesses that she used to walk around with a hypothetical empty cup, asking others to fill it with approval. The problem is that the cup was never full. It had pinholes, and its contents were constantly flowing back out. No amount of compliments, pats on the back, or unbridled admiration could keep it full.

There is someone who can exchange our empty, broken cups for living springs—ones that bubble up from within and flow continuously with fresh water, overflowing and pouring out to those we encounter (see John 4:13–14).

As Carrie reminded me with her teaching, "In Christ, we are *already* approved." I often forget this. Old mind-sets die hard. Carrie explained, "Nothing we do or don't do affects His approval. If we are in Christ, then we are approved through His death and resurrection. We are deemed worthy. We have been examined and found genuine."[4] And it isn't because we've done enough or are enough; it's because Jesus did and is. We can indeed rest from the quest for perfection because He has accomplished what we are striving for.

You can retire from your need to earn God's favor and start to enjoy your inheritance right now, assured of His approval through Christ, because He purchased your freedom from your cell of sin.

Behind door number one, we discover what is ours to possess. It is revealed in the testament bequeathed to us by our Dad. These verses in Ephesians uncover what belongs to us. We are

- adopted through Jesus Christ (1:5)
- redeemed through His blood (1:7)
- forgiven of our sins (1:7)
- made alive with Christ (2:5)
- raised with Christ (2:6)
- seated with Christ in heaven (2:6)
- shown the surpassing riches of His grace (2:7)
- shown kindness from God in Christ Jesus (2:7)
- God's workmanship (2:10)
- created for good works (2:10)
- brought near by Christ's blood (2:13)
- given peace (2:14)
- reconciled to God (2:16)
- given access to the Father (2:18)
- fellow citizens with the saints (2:19)
- members of God's household (2:19)
- being built together into dwellings of God (2:22)

This list represents only a handful of verses in two chapters from just one book of the Bible. I dare you to go on a treasure hunt and uncover more of your inheritance in Christ.

After we know what is ours, we settle into that truth by living it out.

Let's revisit Martha and Mary and take a closer look at a key to freedom we may have missed within this familiar scene: "Only one thing is necessary, for Mary has chosen the good part, which shall not be taken away from her" (Luke 10:42, NASB). The Greek word for "part" in this verse is *meris*. *Meris* means an assigned part, a portion, or a share of the inheritance.[5]

Wow! Mary chose the good part, portion, and share of her spiritual inheritance, and it will not be taken from her. When you look at the word *meris*, it even looks as if it has the word *merry* in it. I don't think it's a stretch to say that there is joy to be found as we choose to possess what's ours in Christ. As daughters, not orphans, we can view this observation in Luke from a place of security. We too can choose to receive our assigned parts and our more-than-enough portions in Christ. We can learn from this verse (about the importance of enjoying what, and who, is ours) and not let it derail us or cause us to deny our wiring.

This whole Martha and Mary thing is more than a matter of personality. It's bigger than being type A or B. Whether you are uptight or laid back, driven or passive, a to-do list gal or a go-with-the-flow woman, you are loved. Regardless of your bent, you face a choice: what to do with the love given and the grace extended to you from your Father, through Christ. Will you live as though it's all up to you, or will you choose to receive your share of the inheritance? Choosing the good part is dependent on knowing that it's good. When you understand the uninhibited love of your Father and the benefits of being a daughter, how can you not choose the better way of resting in who you are in light of who He is?

Jesus invites you to choose what cannot be taken away, washed away, or cut off—to trust Him more than your own ability, to count on God to take care of you as you take care of others, to enjoy your place in the heart of your Dad, who delights in you. It's such a relief to know that we aren't left alone to fend for ourselves (in the kitchen, in the office, or in the kingdom), because Jesus paid the way for our being adopted into God's family and we are home in Him: "Jesus replied, 'Anyone who loves me will obey my teaching. My Father will love them, and we will come to them and make our home with them'" (John 14:23, NIV).

HOME

Our home has its original orange shag carpeting in it. It makes quite a well-worn statement. It puts us and our guests at ease because it's darn near impossible to ruin.

Have you ever been in a home with brand-new light-colored carpet? It looks fantastic, but it's hard to relax because hypervigilance is required to keep it looking that way. Not so with our orange shag! In fact, if you come over, leave your shoes on—it really doesn't matter. We just want you to enjoy yourself.

When Jesus reminded me that He was at home with me, sitting in a comfy recliner in my living room, pressure subsided. For so long, I acted as though He were a guest to impress—one I had to frantically prepare for—instead of family to enjoy. I lived as if my relationship with Him were built on pristine carpeting that required great effort to maintain. But now I can relax within, knowing that our relationship is more like the freedom that comes with the orange shag.

Slaves work to keep the carpet clean at all costs. Daughters rest knowing that their Father is the greatest stain remover of all. The hired help cleans until their hands are calloused, trying to please an unreasonable boss. Orphans strive to find and keep their place. Daughters enjoy the place they already have. They take hold of what's theirs; they don't just admire it from a distance. They honor their Dad by stewarding what He has lovingly entrusted to them.

Being daughters is not an excuse to be lazy but an invitation to delight in what we've been given. Just because the orange shag is hard to ruin doesn't mean I should purposefully spill on it, trying to destroy it. The same is true with the grace we have been given. Just because it's indestructible doesn't mean I should abuse it or take advantage of it. We are compelled to honor our Dad by taking care of what He has faithfully provided. And one day when that shag is exchanged for a luscious chocolaty wood floor, we'll thank God for His provision and give Him credit for the victory.

TIME TO CELEBRATE

Enjoying what is ours is an important principle (from both a spiritual and a practical standpoint). It is called contentment.

It's easy for doers to get one thing done and move right on to the next thing. After I reach a milestone, a friend says to me, "You must be thrilled! Your hard work paid off." My attitude is more like "Finally, that part is done. Now on to the bigger and better thing." My response alerts me to the fact that I haven't taken time to enjoy the moment or celebrate what's already been accomplished. Sometimes I even forget to give thanks to the Lord as I sprint toward the next thing (like the nine healed lepers who didn't return to acknowledge what Jesus had done on their behalf in Luke 17:11–17).

When you have a big goal in sight, it's tempting to keep pushing yourself until you reach your final destination. Although finishing a race is a big accomplishment, each mile run is noteworthy in and of itself. My sister Laura ran her first 25K in college. Alongside thousands of others, our family lined up along the race route to cheer on the runners, celebrating along the way. Proud of Laura's perseverance, I was teary eyed as I watched her run by. Each mile was a step closer to the finish line. Each mile was worthy of celebration (and a gulp of Gatorade).

As I think about all of us crammed on the sidelines in downtown Grand

Rapids, Michigan, cheering on loved ones, Hebrews 12:1 comes to mind: "Since we are surrounded by such a great cloud of witnesses, let us throw off everything that hinders and the sin that so easily entangles. And let us run with perseverance the race marked out for us" (NIV).

Before the revelation of grace, I interpreted this verse to mean "You better watch out. The giants of the faith are keeping a close eye on you. Stay in line and don't trip and fall!" But now I'm convinced that the great cloud of witnesses is more like the crowd gathered at the 25K: wildly encouraging us to keep going, proud of our hard work, acknowledging the determination required, and wanting us to succeed (maybe even throwing confetti our way).

Our Father knows that to finish well we need to pace ourselves. We're on this faith journey for the long run, so let's not ignore our Coach. Regardless of our energy levels, regardless of our ages, regardless of our responsibilities, resting and celebrating are two important bullet points on our to-do lists. But they are not bullets of condemnation. These are line items of delight, not drudgery. God freely supplies gulps of grace as we run (or walk or crawl) this race.

> The people who walked in darkness
>> have seen a great light.
> For those who lived in a land of deep shadows—
>> light! sunbursts of light!
> You repopulated the nation,
>> you expanded its joy.
> Oh, they're so glad in your presence!
>> Festival joy!
> The joy of a great celebration,
>> sharing rich gifts and warm greetings.

The abuse of oppressors and cruelty of tyrants—
    all their whips and cudgels and curses—
Is gone, done away with, a deliverance
    as surprising and sudden as Gideon's old victory over
        Midian. . . .
For a child has been born—for us!
    the gift of a son—for us!
He'll take over
    the running of the world.
His names will be: Amazing Counselor,
    Strong God,
Eternal Father,
    Prince of Wholeness.
His ruling authority will grow,
    and there'll be no limits to the wholeness he brings.
He'll rule from the historic David throne
    over that promised kingdom.
He'll put that kingdom on a firm footing
    and keep it going
With fair dealing and right living,
    beginning now and lasting always.
The zeal of GOD-of-the-Angel-Armies
    will do all this. (Isaiah 9:2–4, 6–7, MSG)

In God's timing and way, we will one day cross the finish line, right into the waiting embrace of our Father, through Christ, our forerunner.

We will then enjoy what's ours in fullest measure—forever. Can you hear the cheers?

Modern Martha · Jami Amerine

Claiming my birthright as daughter has changed so much. I believe God is with me and for me. I no longer embrace the mentality that I have to earn my place next to Him rather than boldly pulling up a chair next to Him, fully invited. When I first started writing, I believed it a fluke, that I didn't deserve to be heard, that I wasn't good enough. Why would He want me? As His daughter, I believe He does want me, unto His death He chose me. This freedom allows me to stop the terror I lived under before and join in the banquet. A celebration for those He adores.[6]

☐ It Is Finished: All Done!

Sometimes on the way to doing more, we rush past what we've already done. Jot down several things you accomplished yesterday. They can be practical or spiritual, big or small, easy or difficult. For example:

- walked the dog
- wrote niece a birthday card
- read Romans 5
- went to physical therapy
- entered a photography contest

Take a moment to celebrate what you have already done instead of fixating on what is left to do. Before bed, record what you did for the day on the "All Done!" calendar (see Bonus Content on the next page) and take a moment to feel good about those things. This can help your brain unwind instead of rev up. Or you may want to try this in the morning before the stress of all there is to do sets in (in this case, record what you did the day before). Take stock of what you've done. Then let your mind rest as you experience satisfaction and a settledness while you go about your day.

Practice being kind to yourself and extending grace as you do this exercise. Don't make light of the little things, as they add up to some really big things. For example, if your "All Done!" calendar is filled with "Changed poopie diapers and fed the baby," wow, that's impressive—you're raising a human! Or if your calendar is filled with "Worked nine to five, went to lunch with a friend, read a book," well done! You're working hard, connecting with others, and learning new things. Some days might look sparse, and others may be bursting at the seams, but regardless, take a beat (or ten) and feel good about what you have achieved.

Bonus Content

Head over to www.katiemreid.com/martha-resources and download a free copy of the "All Done!" calendar. For each day, write down several things you accomplished (not things you need to do but things you already did). At the end of the month, take a moment to celebrate it all. Rejoice in what is already finished.

A Beloved Daughter's Mentality Assessment

Put a check mark by each statement that you find yourself thinking, believing, or acting on. Be honest! Don't check what you *know* is true; put a check by what you are currently *living* as true. This is not the final say on your spiritual state but rather an opportunity to evaluate where you are as you move from a hired-help mentality to a beloved daughter's mentality.

☐ My worth comes from what Jesus has done for me on the cross.

☐ My future is secure in Christ. Nothing can snatch me out of His hand.

☐ Christ can meet all my needs according to His glorious riches.

☐ There is enough of God's love and provision to go around.

☐ I am not left out or left behind by Him.

☐ I believe that God's yeses and nos are for my good.

☐ I can trust others and receive love because I believe that God is trustworthy and loving toward me.

☐ I extend grace to others because I have been shown so much grace by God.

☐ I choose to believe the best about people instead of assuming the worst.

☐ When I fail, I am forgiven by Christ and able to forgive myself with His help.

☐ I celebrate when I succeed and thank God for His goodness, giving Him credit.

☐ I am free to celebrate the success of others because they are not a threat to my position in Christ nor is my position in Christ a threat to theirs.

☐ My behavior does not dull or intensify His love.

☐ I trust God's boundaries for me as safeguards and try to stay within them.

Look back over your answers. Then underline one statement that you have the easiest time living out and circle one that you struggle most to believe. Take some time to talk to God about the two statements. Why do you think it is difficult for you to believe some of these truths? What events, relationships, and circumstances have caused you to doubt these truths? What events, relationships, and circumstances have made it relatively easy to receive these truths? Journal your thoughts, draw a picture, or go for a walk and listen to what He has to say to you, His beloved daughter.

PART III

Standing

Your works are not a
means to keep His love;
they are a response of
gratitude for His love.

7

The Middle Ground Between Striving and Slowing

Stewarding Well Without Overdoing It

෴

Enough is as good as a feast.

—English proverb

The push of independence and the pull of responsibility are a dizzying reality that we face as women. It's the friction between conquering the world and keeping it intact. Conflicting voices bellow from the left and call out from the right, "This is the way you should go."

Experts tell you to strive to make the most of your life. Set goals, work hard, reach new heights, and do more. Earn gold stars, get promoted, and juggle an obscene number of obligations with ease. Be all you can be, and do all you can with the time you have. Heaven forbid you do anything halfway. You can do it all! The sky is no longer the limit!

Soon we discover the untruth of these ambitious mantras and unrealistic mandates.

Working hard comes pretty naturally for us doers, but it gets ugly when we sacrifice relationships and our well-being in an effort to achieve. Chronic illness is rampant, families fall by the wayside, and we are stressed to the max. Something's gotta give, and we hope it's not us, because we have nothing left in our reserves.

We buy into the lie that we should be all things to all people and look good doing it (wearing skinny jeans, dangly earrings, and wedges). We have opportunities like never before as women, yet that doesn't mean we should say yes to every opportunity or grab hold of every new idea we scroll past. Yes, working hard is admirable. Yes, being present with loved ones is wise. But we cannot do it all.

Other experts tell us to slow down and be more present so we don't miss out on our lives. We're supposed to take care of our souls, sleep more, slow down, and do less. We must ignore our ambitions, quit our jobs, and take things off our plates and be happy about it. For doers, working less is unnatural, and it's painful when we short-circuit our wiring in an effort to be accepted.

We are urged not to do too much, not to overpack our schedules, and to be mindful of rest. We can hear the warning sirens from our bodies, if we slow down long enough to listen. While it is important not to overdo it, we don't have to say no to every opportunity or dismiss every invitation that lands in our inboxes. No, we cannot add more hours to the day. No, our worthiness is not based on how productive we are. But there are specific works prepared in advance for us to do (see Ephesians 2:10).

One camp shouts, "Hustle!" Another camp whispers, "Hush." And we are threatened with the reality of burnout or boredom, depending on which camp we choose to pitch our tents in.

More! Less.

Less! More.

Just do it! Just say no.

Strive! Slow.

Rush! Savor.

What's a woman supposed to do (or not do)?

Our heads spin; our resolve wanes. We get rope burn between the yank and tug of these conflicting messages. We feel both the angst and privilege of being women in this day and age.

Some of us have overdone it physically (through overcommitting, indulging in things we shouldn't, running on little sleep, and so on), so we swing too far in the opposite direction to make up for the messes we've found ourselves in. Sometimes we overdo it and need to slow down a bit. Yet some of us are buried under to-do lists that won't get done unless we do them. We may find ourselves in circumstances where more is required than we bargained for. In these cases, getting things done is less about striving and more about surviving.

This tug-of-war between busyness and stillness does a number on me. It wears me out and brings me down. I never feel as though I am hitting the mark. And I find myself at His feet only when I am knocked off mine (from overdoing it).

Many of us aren't sure where the middle ground is anymore, which makes standing on it difficult. But even when we struggle to find the solid ground between striving and resting, we are still adored daughters of a good Father who leads us with love.

BALANCING ACT

When I rush and strive, I can feel as though I'm neglecting my most important relationships. However, when I slow and savor, I often feel lost and edgy, sometimes thrashing like a caged bull behind the starting gate. Yes, there is a time for every activity under heaven (see Ecclesiastes 3:1). A time to work, a time to rest. A time to push through and get things done and a time to sit still and relax. But I'm afraid we've bypassed the middle ground. Somewhere between striving and slowing, between hustling and hushing, between rushing and savoring, there is a clearing. It's called moderation for the modern-day woman. There's a rustic wooden sign that arches above the clearing's entryway, inscribed with *Grace*. It's a place of freedom, a land of abundance, a haven dubbed "enough." It's neither confining nor compromising. It is a lush, inviting space full of love for the doer's heart and rest for the try-hard soul. But many miss out on this sweet spot because they are busy trying to maintain some semblance of balance.

My friend Tyra is a busy mama of six children. She recently posed these thoughts:

> Do you ever bear the weight of caring for your children, meeting your boss' expectations, satisfying your husband in the bedroom, caring for an aging parent, and bringing food to a neighbor who just had a baby? . . . WHEW! . . .
>
> The notion of "balance" summons an image of perfectly executing ALL my responsibilities, ALL in perfect order, ALL the time. It looks like being everything to everyone, doing everything for everyone and looking cute and wearing a smile while doing it. And somehow . . . we've bought into this LIE! . . .
>
> It is unrealistic to believe you have to do ALL things well, ALL at the same time.
>
> Trying to achieve balance can be a fruitless pursuit of an elusive goal.[1]

This elusive goal of balance is something many of us try to achieve, only to find ourselves floundering in seas of fret and regret. We struggle to master the scales and the schedules as we work to find harmony.

One Sunday after church, I asked a friend to pray for me. I often find myself in the midst of work and family demands and don't know how to stay balanced. As my friend poured out her prayer, she mentioned that balance might look different than I thought it did. Her insight caused me to wonder whether my understanding of balance was off kilter.

My definition of balance has been to walk a straight line, not tip the scales too much in one direction or the other, and avoid disapproval by keeping everyone happy. Yet this is unattainable because it is unrealistic. What I am actually trying to achieve is perfection and being everything to everyone—a savior complex, if you will—which is a surefire way to live an unbalanced life.

How do we make sure our priorities are in order? We first ask God to help us relate to Him as daughters, not slaves. We trust our Father's heart toward us as we follow His direction. We stand on His toes as we dance through the day (sometimes spinning with ease, sometimes fumbling, but always cherished). We take off the mantle of being responsible for everyone and everything. We lean into His ability to uphold our days, guide our schedules, and keep the world spinning, even when our schedules feel anything but balanced. We stop trying to complete a "top to bottom list" or live a "compartmentalized life" and begin living an "interconnected life" that relies on Jesus at the center, not Jesus as a lofty goal to reach the harder and faster we pedal toward Him.[2] This kind of life depends on the timeless guidance of the Creator and moves in tandem with His Spirit.

When we realize that the aim isn't to score a perfect ten on the balance beam of life, the quest becomes less about finagling and more about focusing on the tasks at hand. We step off the ladder of self-reliance and ask Him to help us be faithful stewards of what He has entrusted to us. We trade in contention for contentment and lean into His sufficiency. We rest in His ability to sustain us and our schedules too.

When I act as if it's all up to me, I elevate my doer's heart above my dependence on the One who is not served by human hands, as if He needed anything. And I forget that *He* is the One who gives life and breath and everything else (see Acts 17:25). On the other hand, when I downplay what I am called to and capable of, I ignore the reality that His divine power gives me everything I need for life and godliness (see 2 Peter 1:3).

My friend Paula is a passionate musician who gives her all to the task at hand. We were getting ready to rehearse for a women's conference when she confessed she had not prepared as much as usual. I laughed, knowing she probably had still put in hours and hours of preparation. She readily agreed with my estimation. Her boss at work had told her something similar. He observed that Paula's slacking off was equivalent to most people's average effort, which still translated into hard work!

While doing our best is important, there is a slippery slope between excellence and perfectionism. Excellence is honorable; perfectionism is idolatry. It sounds harsh, I know, but let me explain further. I used to wear perfectionistic tendencies like a bedazzling badge, proud of my attention to detail and strong work ethic. However, I eventually realized that being a perfectionist is not endearing. It actually represents a false view of self and a skewed view of the Savior.

Perfectionism declares, "I am counting on myself to be flawless—to reach superhuman status with my talents, time, and resolve. I don't need the Savior to sustain me. If I work hard, I can earn an A+ by giving 110 percent. I am often discouraged in my quest and irritable with others in the process, but I keep going and going and going, trying to prove my worth."

Perfectionism sets its victim up for failure, insisting we can be like God if we work hard enough. This philosophy communicates, "What Jesus did was not enough! I must prove I am enough."

Admitting inability and resting in His ability can be uncomfortable for self-sufficient gals. But we are in jeopardy of missing out on the abundant life when we insist our sanctification is based solely on our productivity. We are in danger of misrepresenting the gospel when we believe that our salvation is dependent on our effort.

There is only one who is perfect: His name is Jesus Christ. We cannot achieve perfection apart from Him, no matter how many hours we log, no matter how hard we labor.

This can be a source of frustration for modern Marthas. You better believe that as a doer I want my work to matter. I don't want all this effort to be for naught. But when I demand perfection from myself and others, it's as if I am berating and negating my Savior—accusing Him of not being enough, not doing enough.

Jesus did not strive or slack off. He obeyed His Father even to death. He kept pace with God's will, not running ahead or lagging behind. He stayed focused on what He had been called to do without overdoing it and was available to those around Him, without underdoing it. He found the middle ground.

What was His secret?

Jesus knew who He was in light of His Father. His Father was enough for Him. And Jesus is enough for us. When we forget our position in Christ as daughters, we have a hard time enjoying spiritual rest as we face life's demands. When this happens, we may find ourselves buried in "do" as we strive to earn what is already ours, or held back by fear, afraid we'll mess it all up and lose what we already possess.

How do we find our way back to peace? How do we kindly invite our souls to take their seats? We do this by recalling what is true, focusing on what has been done, resting in who we already are, and walking out what belongs to us. In other words, we don't have to scrounge up more resolve; instead, we can sink into the plush chair of grace. Peace has *already* made its home in us. Our souls are seated, *once and for all*, with Christ. We release the tension we've been carrying as we breathe in His presence. Even during meal prep, even in the presence of pressing difficulties, even in the middle of the unraveling, our souls lean into unfading truth.

STREETLIGHT STRATEGY

From a practical standpoint, we can make wise decisions by implementing something I call the streetlight strategy. Imagine you are at a busy intersection. You are in a hurry to get home, yet you stop because the light is red. If the light is yellow, you have a choice to make. Do you try to make it through (if you have enough time), or do you brake because you might not make it safely across before the light turns red? Once the light is green, you are on your way again.

We can use this same idea for deciding when to stop, when to slow, and when to go, in regard to adding more to our to-do lists. For example, the other day I was asked to co-chair a committee. I assessed what was already on my plate and realized there was no extra room on it. This was clearly a red-light situation, so I said no. I also could have evaluated whether there was something else I could take off my plate to make room for serving on this committee. In the past I have recklessly added to my already full plate, which has created some sticky situations.

When you find yourself faced with a choice to say yes or no to adding a new responsibility, take stock of the traffic flow in your life at present. Is it wise to proceed, or could it be detrimental to you and those traveling with you?

The committee decision was an easy no, but what about when things aren't as clear? Like when it's dinnertime but there is also a work deadline, unfolded laundry, and a ringing phone? In this case, assess what must be done first. Are there others who can help? Modern Marthas often pride themselves on all they can accomplish, but we don't always need to be the ones to do it all. Call in reinforcements when you can. The art of delegation is a beautiful thing.

What do you do when you find yourself in a season with little to no margin? Maybe you are a single mom or are married but your spouse does not help (or is not able to). Maybe you have a relative in poor health and are his or her support system but you also have a stressful job and a to-do list a mile long. What then? It's as though you are at an intersection with traffic zooming past in all directions yet you must plow forward because your present circumstances demand it; it's a matter of survival. This is the time you send out a distress signal. You let others help. Ambulances with sirens can get through red-light intersections. Who might be able to provide life support during this intense season?

My friend Heidi is the mother of four. Her oldest is a boy, her middle children are twin boys, and her youngest is a girl. Heidi nearly lost her life when pregnant with her youngest three children. She developed HELLP syndrome, and her kidneys were in serious danger of shutting down. Her daughter, Auri, was delivered by C-section at thirty-one weeks. As Heidi and her family waited until her daughter was healthy enough to come home, Heidi traveled three hours round-trip to drop off milk and hold Auri. She was juggling homelife with three active boys and hospital life with her little girl. The house was not picked up, but children were held close. Meals were simple because the schedule was complex. The five-year plan had been replaced by the five-minute plan. Balance for Heidi did not look like a perfectly posed acrobat on a tightrope. If she tried to achieve that standard, she would land in a heap of exhaustion, falling from the heights of unrealistic expectations. Meeting the needs of her family at this juncture looked less like Martha Stewart and more like *Survivor* as Heidi navigated the choppy waters of her circumstances.

When we find ourselves in intense seasons, we often need the support of others to stay afloat. Asking for help or taking others up on their offers to assist is not weakness but wisdom.

Do you have a friend with whom you could swap services? Maybe you have a friend who loves to cook. Could you pay her to make meals for a few weeks, or could you offer to watch her kids one day a week in exchange for her providing you some freezer meals? Enlist a friend to help you tackle what is holding you back from efficiency and margin. For example, my friend Christy has a friend who is an organizing pro. Once a year, Christy's friend comes to stay and whips her home into shape. Christy takes good care of her friend while she is visiting by feeding her and providing fun outings. And her friend eliminates a lot of stress for Christy in the process. These two modern Marthas have doubled their strengths instead of depleting them by finding a trade-off that energizes them both.

So the next time you are trying to decide how to steer your schedule, take stock of the current situation. Is your calendar already jam packed? Is there room to proceed safely? Is there a clear path in front of you? Do you need to ask for help to navigate your next move? Let's not be reckless with our pace or lag when it's time to accelerate.

Let's ask God to guide us as we utilize the streetlight strategy. Then let's enjoy the freedom that comes from confident (not careless) driving.

Red: Stop

Be aware that it is dangerous to continue at your current speed. Stop and wait until traffic clears or call in reinforcements to help you get through this congested season.

Yellow: Slow

Use caution in proceeding. Evaluate whether it is wise to go forward or to stop. Yield before you say yes; pause before you proceed. Take a moment to assess your motivation. Is adding this responsibility a necessity? Are you motivated by guilt or striving to please people? Or is this a good opportunity that you are able to navigate without crashing?

Green: Go

Take note of your surroundings and those in your company as you move forward with confidence. Reevaluate when traffic patterns shift.

JUST SAY YES, NO, OR HELP

As recipients of grace and confident daughters of a loving Father, we are also freed to serve from a place of peace. When asked to do something or when trying to decide what to do next, let's remember

- there is blessing in saying yes to God's assignments
- there is freedom to say no to guilt, manipulation, and trying to prove ourselves
- asking for help isn't weak; delegation and calling in reinforcements can be wise and necessary

Have you been asked to add something to your plate, or is there something on your plate that needs to come off? Look over the abovementioned "yes," "no," and "help" statements and ask God to illuminate which response is best for this situation. You won't always get it right or get it done, but there is grace for that too.

THE MAXIMIZER

My friend Dalene lives in South Africa. Although we live more than eighty-five hundred miles apart, the tendency to overdo it translates across continental divides. By her own admission, Dalene is the type to unbutton her jeans before she closes the bathroom door, just to save time. She doesn't mop the floor without streaming a sermon on her iPad because *just* mopping seems like a waste of time. In checkout lines, she checks emails. If she does something that was not on her to-do list, she jots it down on said list, just for the satisfaction of ticking it off.

According to the Gallup StrengthsFinder assessment, "Maximizer" is one of Dalene's top strengths. She is a big believer that we all have potential—God dreams stitched into our DNA. And we all have time—a fixed number of beats programmed into our hearts. Dalene is passionate about the truth that we need to maximize both time and potential.

But being efficient, energetic, and task oriented can tip a person over to the dark side, where a wound-up woman lurks. Dalene confesses that when she operates in the shadow of her strengths, getting the job done becomes more important than people's feelings, and the fruit of her labor becomes more important than the fruit of the Spirit.

Not too long ago, Dalene wrote two books in two years. All that writing was interspersed with weekend ministry events and blogging and mentoring and the ordinary wonder-struck weariness of being a day-in-day-out mama of two. She was creatively, emotionally, and spiritually depleted. When she reached the last of her deadlines, she decided to take three months off. Her body let out a sigh of relief: *Phew! She is stopping at last!* And then Dalene promptly got shingles, which tends to show up as a kind of after-the-fact, please-rest-already thing. But because she is wired for productivity, resting on the couch while her boys were at school filled her with unrest. Relaxing was stressful for this modern Martha!

Dalene asked God to replenish her in ways that fit her temperament meaningfully. So she painted, even though she was not a skilled artist. She went walking and dancing and invited foodie friends to hang out in her kitchen and teach her to cook scrumptious things. She sought out kind, inspirational people so they could solve many of the world's problems together over cappuccinos. Dalene gardened. She read piles of books—some for grown-ups, some for kids. She prayed. She watched chick flicks. She dated her husband. She learned three chords and two songs on the ukulele. She sang loudly in the car and cleaned out her house and her Dropbox.

When Dalene began organizing her makeup drawer, she rediscovered her grandmother's powder case. After her grandmother had passed away and she and her relatives were going through her things, Dalene asked whether she could have it. It held the fragrance of dear Gran, and opening it was like taking a sip of her childhood.

That powder case wasn't worth much at all. Dalene's grandmother bought it at a drugstore decades ago. But it's precious because it belonged to someone who Dalene dearly loved. She didn't love it because it's worthy; it's worthy because she loved it.

"And it's that way with God," Dalene observed. "He doesn't love you because you are worthy; you are worthy because He loves you. Jesus didn't say, 'I'd better die for *that* woman because We'll definitely get something out of the deal. Let's get her onboard. It'll be [a] win-win. She could really add significantly to Our organization.' He died *despite* the fact that you and I had nothing of real value to bring to the table. His great love attributes worth to us without us doing a thing. We don't have to achieve to be accepted. We're accepted. Period. It's our acceptance that leads to our achievements. And it's a marvelous relief that we don't have to carry the weight of success because all that heavy glory gets handed straight to God."[3]

ALREADY ENOUGH

Instead of piling heaping portions of guilt onto your already full plate, what if you enjoyed the cleansing agent of grace, already at your disposal? Enough is enough! And sometimes good enough is good enough. We don't have to be more or do more or do less or be less to be okay. We are okay—more than okay—through Christ and our acceptance of His completed work on the cross.

We hang up our superhero cape of self-effort and twirl with the robe of righteousness that doesn't come off. We ignore the pointing finger that we must achieve balance *or else*. We gladly receive the good news of grace that is already ours—whether in plenty or in need, in stress or in rest, in sickness or in health.

I'm convinced there is liberation waiting on the flip side of this I'm-every-woman mind-set. We are not the Savior! We can't be. We are not enough. We are in great need of the Great Enough: "He said to me, 'My grace is enough for you, for my power is made perfect in weakness.' So then, I will boast most gladly about my weaknesses, so that the power of Christ may reside in me" (2 Corinthians 12:9, NET).

Because we are strong and confident women, feelings of inadequacy and weakness are not twin sisters we like tagging along. However, these tagalongs are blessings in disguise, as they lead us to the One whose strength is untiring and capability unwavering.

Jesus became flesh and dwelled *among* us so that through His death and resurrection—and our faith in Him—He could dwell *within* us. Our lack of balance (or ability to achieve it) is not cause for guilt but rather an opportunity for grace. We want to honor God with our choices, yet when we slip or throw a fit, we remain loved. Our limitations do not affect His ability to abide within us. Our successes point to His glory. We can rest because perfection is not up to us; perfection is *in* us, and His name is Jesus.

Whether we struggle with balance in our food choices, spending habits, extracurricular commitments, or various roles, it is imperative to remember that we are in right standing with Father God, because Jesus provided the perfection required to redeem us from sin and separation from Him. As author Asheritah Ciuciu said, "Our self-control before that plate of cookies does not make God love us any more or any less than He already does. We must also remember that when we're tempted to turn our healthy eating plan into a legalistic list of dos and don'ts. Our heathy eating doesn't earn God's favor: Jesus already did that for us."[4]

Jesus is enough for our not-enough.

We see throughout Scripture this principle of God's supernatural provision in the midst of human limitation. As Jesus taught the multitudes in Bethsaida about the kingdom of God, it eventually was time to eat. Jesus's disciples suggested that the people (about five thousand men in addition to women and children) find a place to stay and food to eat because they were in a remote location. But Jesus told the disciples to get them something to eat. They were dumbfounded by this directive. I imagine that the doers in the bunch were quickly thinking through all the angles of how to pull off a massive meal—and coming up short. So many mouths to feed, so much food needed, yet all they had was five loaves of bread and two fish.

Then Jesus instructed His disciples, saying,

"Have them sit down to eat in groups of about fifty each." They did
so, and had them all sit down. Then He took the five loaves and the
two fish, and looking up to heaven, He blessed them, and broke them,
and kept giving them to the disciples to set before the people. And
they all ate and were satisfied; and the broken pieces which they had
left over were picked up, twelve baskets full. (Luke 9:14–17, NASB)

In His presence they reclined, and Jesus blessed the meager offering.
Miraculously, it was more than sufficient. They all ate and were filled, and
there were even leftovers! In the middle of a desolate place, God provided
what was needed and then some. He sent the Bread of heaven to be broken
so His wrath for sin would be satisfied. Jesus proved that He is enough—for
our lack, for our sin, for our tendency to overdo or underdo—and that He is
able to supply what we need to manage our daily responsibilities as well.

If you are like me—or the Israelites who wandered in the wilderness—
you need a little help remembering what is true as you exit a life of slavery and
enter a life of royalty.

My motivation for doing used to be driven by an unquenchable need for
approval. I feared being invisible, so I worked hard to be known. But I didn't
just want to be known; I desired to be elevated to star status. I wanted to see
how I fared when compared with others, often calculating where I ranked on
a skewed scale of beauty, brains, and talents as if all of life was a Miss Universe
pageant (minus the swimsuit competition, please!).

In my quest to be the best, I lost sight of the truth.

I strove to be the best but ended up feeling worse. I was drained and running on reserve battery power. I needed to be recharged, straight from the
Source—jolted back to truth, away from the lies that threatened to short-
circuit real living.

UNEXPECTED GIFT

In an effort to find myself, buried beneath real and self-imposed responsibilities and on a mission to recover fragmented parts of a weary heart, I started writing. Under all the words, under all the stories, was someone who needed to be found: a daughter waiting to be reborn.

My husband noticed a transformation as I wrote. A more fully alive version of myself surfaced. I smiled more easily and wasn't bogged down with typical annoyances, because my creativity had a steady outlet. But as my fingers tapped on the keyboard, I started grasping for more and more, trying to fill an insatiable hunger for validation that began when I was a young woman. Under the guise of ministry, sandwiched between good works and moving words, I became a workaholic. And in the process of following a great dream, I was careless with my greater dream of being a devoted wife and attentive mama. Sometimes I even neglected my posts at home for my posts online.

The tension of two callings threatened to snap me in two and sting those closest to me. I was so focused on the result that those dearest to me felt unseen at times. During this workaholic season, I was also training for a half marathon. *Overachiever* is tattooed on my ankle, in Hebrew. Not really, but proving myself has always marked me.

I wandered from home in an emotional and spiritual sense.

I tried to implement some strategies that could improve the situation, but the changes were short lived. It was as though I couldn't help myself—true signs of an addict. I wanted better boundaries, more balance, to not work so hard, to be able to pause in the middle of a project (without resentment), but I didn't know how. My drive to prove landed me in a heap of do. I tried to fix myself, but it didn't stick. I'd tried it my way and made quite a mess.

So one day, on a country road east of our house, I put one foot before the other and reluctantly let God dig up the dirt in my heart as I ran (okay, jogged). From a place of desperation, with some trepidation, I prayed something like this: *God, help! I'm scared to surrender, but I give You the right to control, again. I love You. I want to be made well, even though I don't know what that process might look like. Help me come back to You. Turn my heart home.*

I took a wobbly step back toward Dad, with birds overhead and cornstalks as witnesses.

Not too long after this heartfelt prayer, Adam and I made time for a much-needed getaway near Traverse City, Michigan. We dispersed our (then) four children to various family members so we could celebrate our anniversary and reconnect after an exhausting summer of moving and ministry. It wasn't convenient to get away, because it required lots of mental space and preparation. Like a college student who is done with exams but must remind herself that she doesn't have to study anymore, I took a few days to remember how to relax. It was wonderful to have time with Adam, no other responsibilities, just enjoying each other's company. It was as if we were newlyweds again.

We had always talked about having five children. God had miraculously brought our fourth child, Isaiah, to us through adoption, and he was then almost two and a half. We were planning on adopting again. But in an unbridled moment of trusting God no matter the outcome and declaring that He knew best, I found myself expecting shortly after our getaway. A beautiful plot twist! God knew just what I needed to be made well. Funny, because I sure felt sick during the first trimester.

God answered my roadside prayer in a most unexpected way, with a miracle. He responded to my need for restoration with new life. A pregnancy.

Our fifth child. And guess what? When you're pregnant, you go to bed earlier. You nap freely. You preserve your energy because you want to care for the little one developing within. You slow down because you're concerned for another.

God turned my heart home.

While I was a long way off, He saw me. He could have reprimanded me for straying, but instead, He met me there, mightily, in the middle of the mud, with grace. He didn't hold me at arm's length but wrapped me up tight. He treated me as a daughter, not the hired help. He gave me a gift when I deserved punishment. He provided forgiveness when I admitted I was unable to pull myself away from the pen. And if that weren't enough, He went so far as to provide new life.

Thousands of years ago, God's people longed for a King to rule and reign and establish peace on their behalf. God answered their cries by sending them a baby, and many of them missed the answer because they expected Him to provide in a different way. Jesus was more than the King of the Jews; He was the King of kings, who came to restore the people to their heavenly Father. Sin had separated them from God, but He made the way for them to come home, both on earth and for eternity. We return not through works, not through good behavior, not through prayers morning, noon, and night but through the way, the truth, and the life: Jesus. Only Jesus.

And He did not come for just the Jews; He came for all of us. He died and rose that you might have new life, no longer branded by sin, no longer an orphan but a daughter. It's so simple and so unbelievable at the same time. We deserve punishment, yet He offers a gift instead.

As you move from swiveling to sitting, from striving to abiding, from a hired-help mentality to a royal daughter's reality, may the following "already enough" statements help you combat guilt for overdoing it or underdoing it in areas of your life. May these truths help you focus on what is already yours because your position in Christ is secure. And may they reiterate that Christ is already enough whether you find yourself in a desolate or spacious place, a hungry or satisfied state, a harried or hushed season.

- My value is not based on how well I perform. Christ has performed flawlessly and determined my value through His creation of me and His sacrifice for me (Genesis 1:27; Psalm 18:30; Matthew 10:31; John 3:16).

- I don't have to prove my worth by overcommitting. Christ already proved my worth by dying for my sins (Romans 5:8).

- Just because I am good at something does not mean I am obligated to say yes. Christ has specific assignments for me just as God had specific assignments for Christ (Ephesians 2:10).

- Even when I act unrighteously, God's righteousness remains on and within me because of my faith in Christ's permanent work of salvation (Romans 1:17; 2 Corinthians 5:21; 1 John 2:1).

- When my offering seems meager and my resources are lacking, God can miraculously multiply and supply more than enough for the need at hand (Luke 9:16–17; Philippians 4:19).

- God's love for me does not fluctuate based on whether I do too much or not enough. Through Christ's doing enough on the cross and my belief in Him, I am loved and in right standing with God (Romans 8:33, 38–39).

Revisit these "already enough" statements as often as necessary to help you enjoy your security in Christ (or visit www.katiemreid.com/martha -resources to access a printable or digital version).

Modern Martha **Jen Weaver**

I've come to understand there is really no such thing as balance. The minute I think I have something balanced, something else shifts in my life. ... There is always something that's changing. I just work to hold it all very loosely, and I ask God to help me do the things that He wants me to get done in the day, and I trust Him with it all. And some days it works out amazingly, and I feel like a rock star ... and then there are other days, and it's just a mess. ... I hold on to [grace] not only to give that to other people, but I hold on to that for me. The Lord has grace upon grace for me and I need it. I can give myself grace upon grace because I'm learning too. I'm figuring this out. I've never been in this season [before], and thankfully, God has grace.[5]

☐ It Is Finished: **Permanently**

Identify and write down areas in your life where you're struggling to find the right balance between striving and slowing, and then write applicable truths from Scripture (found on the "already enough" list) near them to remind you that Christ's forgiveness and love are permanently available to you.

8

Easy Does It

Rest for the Try-Hard Soul

೧

Spiritual rest is not a place, but a person and
His name is Jesus.

—Holly Haynes

find myself with a rare moment in which my motivation to clean the
house and the time available to do so align. I'm determined to subdue
the mess with a vengeance. I start off strong, dramatically dumping all the
clothes out of my dresser and onto the floor. I refold the items and reorganize
each drawer so that it closes with ease. All is as it should be (cue a contented
sigh).

Wait! I'm sorry. That's not exactly how it happens.

Halfway through Operation Tidy Up the Drawers, I go into the bathroom and discover that it needs a good cleaning, so I stop said dresser project
and start degrossifying the bathroom. As I am swishing the toilet with vigor,

I hear piercing screams coming from my frustrated toddler. As I tend to Isaiah, I walk past Brooke's room and notice piles of books that have made their way off the shelves and all over her floor—the floor with traces of glitter nail polish from a rest time gone bad. I carry whimpering toddler into big sister's room, and we start reshelving the books. In a fleeting moment of insanity, I consider how satisfying it would be to put all the books in alphabetical order. But "ain't nobody got time for that!" At least not today.

The stress mounts as my half-finished projects pile up . . . and then I hear a flush. *Oh no!*

"Don't use that toilet! I was in the middle of swishing!" I yell (from the room with the books that are now partway on the shelves and definitely not in alphabetical order). The kids are exasperated as I shout conflicting orders.

"Line up the shoes, please. And quick!" I say to my son Banner, who is playing a handheld video game.

"Huh?"

"Son!"

"Okay, okay. Just a minute."

"And you, Kale! Stop hiding in your room. Go hang the coats up. How many times do I have to—?"

"Mom!"

"What?"

"You're beautiful," Kale coos.

His compliment stops my tirade. "Why, thank you, son. That's so nice—Wait! Wait a minute. I see what you're doing here. You're trying to distract me from dishing out more chores!"

"What do you mean?" he says with a sly grin.

He's done this before—this transforming-my-foul-mood-with-kindness thing. It usually works, but not today. I'm cranky. I just want a clean house. Is that too much to ask?

"Come and swish the other toilet, Banner. And did you take out the recycling yet? Hurry up!"

"Mooomm, you already asked me to do the shoes. I can't do shoes, swishing, and recycling at the same time."

"Brooke, why are you reading? We're supposed to be putting the books away. We don't have time to read right now!"

"Fiiinne! Why are you in such a bad mood, Mom? Sheesh!"

"Mommy, I need a Band-Aid," whimpers Isaiah.

"Let me see. Nope, you don't."

"Yes, I dooo-uh!"

Golly, would you look at the time! Time to scrounge up lunch. I'm hungry and so is my brood! My motivation to clean has long since flown out the unwashed window. And now I have a bigger mess on my hands than when I began my noble quest. *Sheesh!*

Now, if I could just concentrate on one thing at a time, as sister Mary did, I might not find myself in this predicament.

But seriously, whether you have too many tabs open on the home screen or you are a meticulous, one-thing-at-a-time kind of gal, it takes discipline and preparation to rest well.

It can be hard to focus on the same thing for an extended period when there's just so much to do.

WHY IS IT SO HARD?

We've talked a lot about resting in our position in Christ. We've established that we are loved as we are and that we don't have to "do" to gain what we already possess in Him. Our value is secure; our salvation is sealed. It's almost time to start serving from a place of strength, not stress. *Can't wait! Bring it!*

But first we pause to address the importance of rest—not just spiritually but physically as well. We all know that sleep is important, and most likely we aren't getting enough of it. *Yawn.* Modern Marthas often strive to get their lengthy to-do lists done but face frustration as the list grows, the schedule fills, and energy is spent.

Can you relate to these reasons why it might be so hard to rest?

- You juggle so many things that you're afraid you might drop something if you slow down.
- You feel guilty about letting yourself rest.
- Someone always seems to need something from you.
- You avoid hurt by staying busy.
- There are tasks to be done that won't get done unless you do them.
- You aren't sure whether you're resting "right."

Sometimes we need to do *more* work ahead of time so we can more fully enjoy our downtime!

When Adam and I got married in June 2001, I created a nine-page wedding agenda. I wanted to think through every detail so everyone knew what was expected, so things would go as smoothly as possible, and so I could relax on our wedding day and not spend it answering tons of questions. While I may have gotten made fun of for the typed-up play-by-play, it made for a delightful day.

When a teacher knows she will be absent, she creates lesson plans for the sub. However, there are times the effort it takes to prep for a break doesn't seem worth it. Sometimes we stress about rest because resting from all there is to do can feel like *another* thing to do!

As I admitted on the massage table in chapter 3, rest can be tricky for modern Marthas. We often must work at relaxing, because it doesn't come naturally for doers like us. It can be difficult to rest when we find ourselves partway through projects, in between jobs, caring for our kids and our aging parents, or smack-dab in the middle of arguments.

Excuses not to rest are everywhere!

I'll rest when life slows down.

I'll take a vacation after I meet this deadline.

When the test results come back, I'll stop worrying.

After I'm married, I won't fill my calendar to the brim.

Once we're out of this rental, we can settle down.

I'll go to sleep after five more minutes of scrolling.

After the kids are grown, we can get away. I promise.

When I get my list done, I'll sit down with you.

If we wait for ideal circumstances and atmosphere, we may never get around to truly resting.

OPENING THE GIFT

Beyond our to-do lists, there is that bigger issue that can keep modern Marthas from resting: a lack of trust. It manifests itself in the form of those pesky worries that swarm overhead. Can you hear 'em buzzing, "What if? What if?"

"What will happen if I let go?"

"What will I miss if I pull away?"

"How will everything get done if I take a break now?"

"What if there is an emergency I can't attend to?"

"What if in the stillness and quiet, I have to face what I've been avoiding?"

When we think that God is withholding good things from us, wants to rob us of fun, and is eager to punish us, we miss the essence of His heart toward His children. When we have an overarching view of God as one who can't be trusted, it distorts our view of rest. Then rest becomes another thing to do or another thing to get wrong. And then we feel lousy again as we compare ourselves with the Mary Club, whose members seem to have the resting and sitting-at-Jesus's-feet thing all figured out.

God rested after six days of creating, and He set that pattern for us too. He knew we needed rest. He designed our bodies to require sleep and a break from our work (see Mark 2:27).

Just like in childbirth, our bodies need time to recover from the strain of labor. Restoration can be slow going when we overdo things.

I was several months pregnant with my first literary baby when I hit a wall. Burning the midnight oil, writing into the wee hours, and getting only sixish hours of sleep while trying to love my man and raise our kids was a recipe for burnout.

One day our three big kids needed to be picked up from Vacation Bible School, but I barely had the energy to walk from my van to their classrooms. I had pushed myself too hard for too long—accelerating past the warning signs—and was reaping the consequences. With slow, deliberate steps, I made it up the bustling stairway. On the verge of collapse, I leaned against a concrete wall. I hoped no one would stop and talk to me, because I wasn't sure I had the energy for that. I felt hollow, as if my body weighed nothing (which is a stretch in light of my birthing hips and substantial thighs). I willed my kids to hurry up so we could get home as soon as possible.

Upon our return, I stayed in bed most of the day, sick from sleep deprivation.

I recognize that although I'm a doer, I haven't been given large doses of physical energy. I usually expend it creatively, not necessarily physically. Ever since my first child was born, afternoon quiet times have been mandatory. I realize that this is a luxury of being home with my kids, but if I don't have some time to rest, I end up sore and grouchy by early evening.

In a moment of bravery, I worked up the courage to ask a mentor what her methods were for getting so much done while she was in the throes of raising a family, because my strategies (or lack thereof) were not working out so well. I was curious to learn how she managed all her responsibilities when she was my age. I sat on the edge of the couch, eager to discover a few tried-and-true techniques from another modern Martha.

"I didn't sit down," she offered.

Oh no. This can't be it.

My shoulders sank, but I tried to mask my discouragement. Considering my workload and energy levels, not sitting down wasn't a good option for me—physically, emotionally, and most definitely not spiritually. But through the filter of my insecurity, I twisted her words to mean that if I didn't do things the same way she did, then I wasn't measuring up as a woman. Not true, I know. Her words were meant to motivate, but what I heard was the sharp whistle of the do-more-be-more train as it raced toward me.

The recollection of this memory leads to an important point: even as doers, we have different capacities and tactics for thriving as modern Marthas. What works for you might not work for me, and vice versa. This is especially true when it comes to rest. But regardless of our differences, rest is a universal human need. Our bodies may require more or less of it, depending on numerous factors, but one thing is for sure: rest is a necessity we can't afford to ignore.

I have tried to downplay my need for it and ended up depleted.

While I think we can all agree that rest is crucial to our well-being, it also can be exhausting to feel guilty that we aren't getting enough of it, according to the experts. Can we please kick guilt to the curb and reframe the conversation? We grab hold of the good news of grace and unwrap its contents with sheer delight. The same is true for rest. It is a gift to be freely enjoyed, not a punishment inflicted on us. When we are young, we nap. We don't always like to do it, but we need it. We fall apart without it.

When our children need something, we do everything we can to meet their needs. Let's say your son needs a pair of shoes. You search for a pair that will meet his need and make him smile. You bring home a pair just his size, but a puzzling thing happens. He chooses not to open the box. He sets it down and never opens it.

What if your daughter has a cavity? She is in pain yet refuses to let you take her in for the necessary treatment. She kicks and screams, even though the procedure would significantly improve her quality of life. Getting a filling might not be pleasant at the time, but it is able to alleviate great discomfort long term.

Do you have a need yet haven't opened the gift that has been provided for your benefit? Is your body in pain or your mind in a constant state of stress, yet you refuse to undergo what is necessary to get back on track? I have been foolish and stubborn when it comes to rest. I have discounted the gift and refused its benefits, viewing it as punishment instead of provision.

Rest is an opportunity to exercise faith that we will be taken care of in the absence of our "doing." It is an opportunity to renounce the hired-help mentality and walk out the beloved daughter's reality.

God knows what we need even better than we do. He does not sleep on the job. He does nothing halfway. He lovingly created us to do, but we also must have sleep and a break. Our needs point to His ability to provide. Our tipping point is an opportunity for Him to show up, break through, and supernaturally provide when there is no other way.

Resting in who He is and who we are in light of Him might not translate to a full night's sleep as we face difficulties. Rest might be a life-giving gasp of air after you've been swimming in the depths for too long. Rest might be receiving grace instead of bullying yourself when you've overdone it or underdone it. Rest might also look like crawling into the comfy recliner with Jesus instead of dusting (yes, definitely instead of dusting).

As we realize that grace trumps law in the area of rest as well, we begin to see the possibilities and not the limitations, the joy and not the duty of it.

I used to think that rest had to look a certain way. But even in my own household, we rest in different ways. One sleeps as long as possible in a dark room. Another one likes to draw, read, and be creative to unwind. I prefer a twenty-minute power nap and then time to think and process while sitting in sunshine. My husband likes to connect with God while in the hunting blind, taking in the sights and sounds of woodland creatures and rugged terrain. Some of my friends like to connect with God by going for a run. This act of exertion calms their minds and rejuvenates their bodies.

Rest can look a thousand different ways. Whatever you choose, may it recharge you, not drain you. Take a break from your work and make room to enjoy things (and people) that you may have been hurrying past. May your time of rest demonstrate the trust you have in God, who gives to His children good gifts, one of those being rest.

Need some ideas to help you unwind?

- Slow down enough to really taste your food.
- Observe the scenery around you. Take notice of the intricacies painted into the landscape of creation.
- Laugh freely with a friend over something silly.
- Go barefoot. Feel the sand, grass, or concrete beneath your feet.
- Hold a conch shell to your ear and listen to the "ocean."
- Smell the mixed bouquets in the grocery store.
- Sit in a hammock with a loved one.

Still need more convincing about rest, from one doer to another? I have personally found it to be true that rest helps me be more productive. As I take a break, it provides space in my schedule and restores my stamina. And it doesn't negate my wiring either; it just places a healthy boundary on it. Doing less can help me gain more—more energy, more creativity, more joy. So there's that. God really does know what He's doing.

STOP! HAMMOCK TIME

Almost every Wednesday night at 9:00 p.m., Adam and I stop what we are doing and climb into a hammock together. From that place of togetherness, we broadcast live about marriage, random silliness, and lessons we have learned along the way. When it gets too cold or dark to be outside in the hammock, we host the show in front of our fireplace.

Wednesday is right in the middle of the week, and we are often tired and sometimes annoyed with each other before we go live. But as we take a weekly break from the busyness of life, we find that the laughter and fun change our outlook and strengthen our relationship. We kick back for about twenty minutes and invest in our marriage through this consistent connection. And the same is true of our relationship with Christ. Connectivity is not often convenient, but it is a powerful tool, crucial to our well-being. Engaging with those around us is becoming a thing of the past as we race to the next thing and text our way through meetings and Meetups (and even vacations).

We've been given so much, yet we hurry past our blessings as we bebop our way to and fro and burn daylight with overcommitment. Let's not grab for more when we're already full. Rest and contentment are close cousins. We don't want to miss out on what's in front of us by looking to the left or the right (or diving too deep into the sea of Facebook). Let's rest assured that God is working even when we're not. I'm afraid that in our scrolling to see what we have missed, we've overlooked the richness of what we already have.

The hammock is waiting. A cocoon of material invites you to nestle in and be held. It's like a sophisticated cradle for big kids and grown-ups alike—space to be soothed, gently rocked back and forth. When you sleep, your body works to repair itself. And when you respond to your Father's invitation to rest under His care, you acknowledge His ability to heal what's broken, help you enjoy what's yours, and prepare you for what's next. Your physical need for rest is a tangible, continual reminder that you are not only a doer but also a daughter.

No more stalling. No more aimless pacing. No more avoiding. Rest is on my to-do list.

Today I choose to respond instead of push. I resist the urge to avoid the haven tucked between the pines. Like Lucy in Narnia, I follow Aslan's whisper on the wind, through a figurative sanctuary of cherry blossoms and bowing birch. I'm quiet enough to hear God's soothing voice.

> Are you tired? Worn out? Burned out on religion? Come to me. Get
> away with me and you'll recover your life. I'll show you how to take a
> real rest. Walk with me and work with me—watch how I do it. Learn
> the unforced rhythms of grace. I won't lay anything heavy or ill-fitting
> on you. Keep company with me and you'll learn to live freely and
> lightly. (Matthew 11:28–30, MSG)

When you RSVP to this kind invitation, you communicate a posture of trust in the One who created the earth and holds it (and you) together. Will you accept His gracious offer? No need to worry about how often you've turned Him down before—this is a guilt-free zone.

Come, daughter. Sit awhile. The dishes can wait. The dusting is negotiable. Your list is not the boss of you. In this moment, take a breather.

Sure, there is more for us to do, good and important things, but we can be at peace in Jesus's presence because we are held by Him. What we lack, He provides. When we miss the mark, He loves us still. When we can't find the way home, He meets us in our place of need. He doesn't ask us to erase our temperament, but He asks us to entrust ourselves to Him (our doer hearts *and* our daughter souls).

He is within us, nearer than our next heartbeat.

Rest is not something we muster up; it's something we melt into. We recall who Jesus is. We settle into what's true. We remember what He has already done. We trust Him with what's undone. We climb into the hammock.

IT'S DEFINITELY NOT QUIET
ON THE WESTERN FRONT!

In college I became more serious about my faith. While home on break, I was in my basement bedroom, with all the lights off, listening to Michael W. Smith's song "I'll Lead You Home." I was trying hard to get in the zone and let the lyrics wash over my soul, ushering me into God's holy presence. All of a sudden, the light turned on as my mom came down the basement stairs to do laundry. I freaked out.

"I am *trying* to connect with the Lord here! I need quiet!" I yelled. My mom pointed out that my response wasn't exactly Christlike.

She was right, although I couldn't see it as clearly then as I do now. There was a disconnect between my walk and my talk. I insisted on a tranquil environment to worship (and treated my family like dirt in the process). *Well, that stinks!*

Although I've matured over the years, I still wrestle to find that undisturbed place of quiet to commune with God. But as a mom of five active kiddos, I don't find it very often. I can let this fact keep me from spending time with Christ, or I can learn to connect with Him amid the crazy.

Our spiritual, emotional, and physical health is stunted when we insist we can't rest unless our relationships, environments, and bodies are in good working condition. There must be a way to rest even when conditions aren't ideal.

Rest is something we practice right where we are. But I'm quickly realizing that it's not very often I will get the quiet basement or a blissful beach. I want to discover how to relax even when it's loud, things are out of my control, and my to-do list is bossing me around. I want to learn to rest in Christ, even in the chaos. I don't want to resent the interruptions. And yelling angry words like "Hey, can't you see I'm trying to serve God here!" falls on deaf ears as the kids return to video games, reading, not napping, and trying to decide which chores they are supposed to complete first.

It's in that place of tension that I bump into the truth that I've been groping for in the dark. Like a light bulb turning on overhead—*Eureka!*—I discover that spiritual rest is not a location but a position, not condemnation but an invitation, not arriving but appreciating what and who is already mine.

We don't have to become someone else or someone more to experience spiritual rest; we just need to remember what is already true. This sounds much easier than what I've been trying.

Modern Martha Amy Elaine Martinez

I only know one place to go when I get that wound up. Relief is waiting in the Presence of God. The problem, once there, I can't seem to unwind enough to fully engage. Screaming thoughts drown out the Voice that calms my weary soul.

How do I truly unwind and really relax?

It seems counter-intuitive, but I run; I run until I reach the place that sets my heart at ease. I press in until I'm satisfied. It's there that I find myself easing into His Presence. In the pursuit, the pantings of my heart become the worship of my soul. It's there I find safety. Finally able to relax and trust, He quiets my heart.[1]

☐ It Is Finished: No More Guilt

On this side of grace, there is so much freedom with what rest looks like. It's not something to search for but Someone to be with. Resting can take on many different forms. The point is to take a break from your typical routine and do something that helps you feel rejuvenated. So whether you put your feet up or your feet hit the pavement for a vigorous run, let's put distance between us and guilt as we relax and refocus in ways that work for us.

What is your favorite way to rest? Schedule time for it this week.

9

Sit Down as You Stand Up

Living Settled Even When You're Busy

ॐ

Peace: It does not mean to be in a place where
there is no noise, trouble, or hard work; it means to
be in the midst of those things and still be calm in
your heart.

—Unknown

I am heading to a gathering of women hosted by my friend Lee. Scheduled to arrive after dinner, I contemplate grabbing a quick bite to eat as I make the two-hour trip. This may seem insignificant, but there is much more involved with it.

To further explain, let me back up to a mission trip to Cambodia that my daughter and I were planning to go on. I felt nervous about our safety, the trip schedule, and how often we would eat. I talked these issues over with a friend who had traveled there many times. She reassured me I'd be fine. I wondered where these concerns were coming from. Was I so accustomed to

American comforts that I had become an inflexible wimp? There might be some truth to that, but my anxiety was more deeply rooted.

Feeling apprehensive about an overseas trip may be normal, but why in the world am I worried about whether I will have dinner in America, at this gathering of friends? God shows me that I often worry about whether my needs will be met in the way I want them to be and therefore take matters into my own hands. While some may label this habit of looking out for my-self as responsible behavior, He reveals there is more going on here. I often don't wait to see how something will turn out before I utilize my know-how and ward off my what-ifs by taking care of myself instead of being at the mercy of another.

While driving to meet my friends, trying to decide whether I should stop for food, I feel as if God says, "Why don't you do a little experiment and trust others and Me to take care of your needs? I can take care of it (and you) even better than you can. Test Me in this and see what I'll do."

Not five minutes after I arrive, Lee asks whether I'm hungry and would like some dinner. It takes a little courage to answer yes, but as I do, she happily pulls out a delicious feast the group had eaten earlier. There are plenty of leftovers! And wouldn't you know? It's one of my favorite meals: grilled-chicken fajitas with all the fixings, complete with authentic-style tortilla shells, fresh guacamole, a quinoa salad (similar to the one I typically order at my favorite coffee shop), and a perfect can of ice tea/lemonade. I smile. "Test Me in this, indeed!" There's even 72 percent cocoa dark-chocolate squares in large supply—simply heavenly.

God shows off as a trustworthy Dad throughout this gathering of His girls. He does such a better job of providing than I could have or would have. How many times have I nearly missed (or totally missed) a lavish spread of His love because I insisted on handling things myself? How often have I eaten a buck's worth of greasy fries, when a feast of goodness was being prepared? How frequently have I forfeited what is mine for a temporary fix that will leave me wanting (like Esau, who sold his birthright to his brother, Jacob, for a pot of stew in Genesis 25:29–34)?

I realize that there are needy people all over the world and that their provision might not look like chicken fajitas or chocolate squares. But it might look like a friend showing up when they're ready to give up, treatment given for troubling symptoms, or rain for crops when the ground is dry.

Father God's care for you may show up in countless ways that are easy to miss if you aren't looking for them: a timely scripture to calm you in a moment of panic, a canceled meeting that lightens your schedule, a joke to amuse you when you're taking life too seriously, peace that fills you, even when it makes no earthly sense, given your situation.

No, He is not a Santa Claus God, but He is a loving Dad who knows best, who knows how to care for us, whether we find ourselves in seasons of deep need or great abundance or wandering somewhere in between. He provides manna for the moment, but so often we try to fill our faces, crunch numbers, or make a way for ourselves instead of waiting to see how He will come through.

Can God provide via a quick trip to the drive-through? Of course. Can He produce sweet fruit even when we feel weathered and withered? Absolutely. But the point is, sometimes do-it-all gals don't leave much room for their Dad to show up and show off.

Maybe Jesus would have provided for Martha's meal with an endless supply of loaves and fish, as He did on the hill with the five thousand. Or maybe He had a savory slice of peace ready for her to partake of, even while she worked hard to prepare the meal for her guests. Whether His provision is practical or spiritual, God is more than able to supply wherever there is lack.

Whether that is at your work, in your marriage, as you parent, in your community, or in the wake of tragedy, God can do anything. Nothing is too hard for Him.

As we talked about in chapter 7, it's okay to ask for help. Calling in reinforcements is wise (unless, of course, you're just being lazy, which I highly doubt since your middle name is Capable). It's not weak or selfish to allow others the joy of easing your load. This is part of God's provision for His doer daughters, and a picture of His body, the church, working side by side, stronger and better together.

My friend Kris Camealy shares about a time she chose to receive in the midst of pressing work:

> The other day I got an email from a woman I did not know, offering
> to bring dinner for my family. I thought about it, prayed about it, and
> wrestled with my fears over accepting her offer, because you know,
> #Strangerdanger. As I debated over what to do, I was reminded that
> hospitality isn't just about giving but also receiving—it's also about
> letting others give of themselves and be a blessing. And when this new
> friend showed up, with a bountiful box full of a complete dinner for
> the 6 of us? I was completely humbled. Her offering came because she
> is also attending #Refine Retreat [the event I host] and she imagined
> that in the midst of the last minute details I'm working on, I could use
> a night off from cooking this week. She was right, and God knew I'd
> need her gracious generosity. If you're more comfortable giving than
> receiving, let me encourage you to accept the offers when you know
> you should. Let someone have the joy of blessing you.[1]

When we learn to receive, we circumvent self-reliance without compromising our God-given capabilities.

MARTHA'S TRANSFORMATION

In the midst of her stress, Martha questioned Jesus: "Lord, do You not care that my sister has left me to do all the serving alone? Then tell her to help me" (Luke 10:40, NASB).

We see Martha's hired-help mentality surface when she questioned the goodness of the Lord: "Lord, do You not care?"

Have you ever asked this of Jesus? I know I have. "Lord, don't You care about _____? If You do, why don't You do something about it?"

Martha also said, "My sister has *left me* to do all the serving *alone*." This also plays into the orphan mind-set of being ignored or abandoned by others—a weary I-guess-it's-all-up-to-me and I've-been-left-all-alone outlook. I totally get Martha's frustration, but on this side of grace, we know that Jesus has not left us to fend for ourselves, even in stressful circumstances. He is with us and for us.

Jesus's words moved Martha from an orphan mind-set to her identity as a chosen daughter when He said, "Mary has chosen the good part, *which shall not be taken away from her*" (verse 42, NASB). We discussed how those with the hired-help mentality fear that what they have will be taken away from them and that someone else will get what they want. Jesus both exposed where Martha struggled and encouraged her to leave that way of thinking behind. We learned earlier that Mary chose to partake of her share of the inheritance in Christ. And Martha had her own share available to her, but it was up to her to choose it for herself.

Martha wasn't the only one in Scripture who exhibited an orphan mind-set. In John 11:48, we read about the chief priests and Pharisees meeting together and trying to decide what to do with Jesus in light of the miracles He was performing: "If we let him go on like this, everyone will believe in him, and the Romans will come and take away both our place and our nation."

The fear of losing position and what we already possess is a sure sign of the hired-help mentality. But that's not where we have to camp out.

After Martha's brother, Lazarus, died, Martha went to Jesus and said, "Lord, if you had been here, my brother would not have died" (verse 21). During this exchange with Jesus, Martha exercised great faith, declaring that Jesus being present could have changed even the most drastic of circumstances. She moved from feeling "left" and "alone" to acknowledging that "God with us" can make all the difference. Jesus went a step further and helped Martha understand.

> You don't have to wait for the End. I am, right now, Resurrection and
> Life. The one who believes in me, even though he or she dies, will live.
> And everyone who lives believing in me does not ultimately die at all.
> Do you believe this? (verses 25–26, MSG)

May we, like Martha, answer "Yes!"

We don't have to wait until we have a two-hour block of quiet time. We don't have to wait until life is neat and tidy. We don't have to wait until the test results come back. Until the bills are paid. Until the conflict is resolved. Until we settle down. Until we take communion. We don't have to wait until Easter morning. We have access to Jesus right here, right now. I AM, the Resurrection and the Life, is present with us! He was there in the past, He will continue to there be in the future, and He is with you now—in joy and sorrow, in life and death. Do you believe this?

> That's why I don't think there's any comparison between the present
> hard times and the coming good times. The created world itself can
> hardly wait for what's coming next. Everything in creation is being
> more or less held back. God reins it in until both creation and all the

creatures are ready and can be released at the same moment into the glorious times ahead. Meanwhile, the joyful anticipation deepens. (Romans 8:18–21, MSG)

Soul rest is found in salvation—in the dying done for us and within us. Spiritual freedom is found in resurrection—in the rising done for us and within us.

We rise as doers, in strength and peace, because we are seated as daughters. Or to put it another way, we sit down as we stand up! We go about the Father's business and work hard for the Lord because we are convinced of His love for us as beloved daughters. Our souls can be at rest even when our hands are busy working.

Six days before the Passover, Jesus therefore came to Bethany, where Lazarus was, whom Jesus had raised from the dead. So they gave a dinner for him there. Martha served, and Lazarus was one of those reclining with him at table. (John 12:1–2)

We often rush to verse 3, about Mary pouring perfume on Jesus's feet, but when we do, we miss some key points found in verses 1 and 2. After Jesus revealed the scope of His true identity to Martha, she was still found serving. You know what this tells me? Martha was made to "do"! Before and after the revelation of who Jesus really is, she was working—first from a place of striving, with a hired-help mentality, and then from a place of settledness, as a beloved daughter. Jesus did not point out that Martha should adjust her attitude as she served here in verse 2. He didn't say that she was worried and distracted again. And He made a point of including the fact that Martha was serving. I think this is a wink from Him to us—a stamp of approval for us modern Marthas. "Your serving is not the issue. In fact, serve on! Serve as a response to knowing who I really am and being loved by Me."

What kindness for Jesus to include us like that in this passage about worship. Little sister Mary wasn't the only one worshipping here; so was big sis Martha. She worshipped Jesus by choosing to believe who He is and then responding to that truth through good works.

Let's not forget newly brought-back-to-life brother Lazarus, who was *reclining* at the table with Jesus. A Jewish speaker told me that this sort of reclining means to lay your head on the chest of the one seated beside you. Lazarus's posture is a picture of soul rest—leaning on the strength of Jesus, his friend, who would soon be providing the blood for the Passover meal with His very life: the Lamb of God without spot or defect. As miraculous as Lazarus's resurrection was, it was a shadow of what was to come.

Prior to His work on the cross, Jesus sat on a donkey's colt as the crowds cried out, "Hosanna!" (John 12:13), which is an exclamation of adoration that means "Oh, save!"

Soon after this event, Jesus died for the sins of the world, answering the cries of our souls. He then rose again from the dead, fulfilling His words to Martha (and us all): "I am the resurrection and the life. Whoever believes in me, though he die, yet shall he live" (11:25).

Post-Resurrection, we are not left to fend for ourselves, because we have assistance of the supernatural variety, in the form of the Holy Spirit. "I will ask the Father, and He will give you another Helper, that He may be with you forever; that is the Spirit of truth, whom the world cannot receive, because it does not see Him or know Him, but you know Him because He abides with you and will be in you. I will not leave you as orphans; I will come to you" (14:16–18, NASB).

The one true God is ever present, and He never lacks or leaves us lacking. It's as though He has a seat in our midst—always attentive, always enough.

The LORD within her is righteous;

> he does no wrong.

Morning by morning he dispenses his justice,

> and every new day he does not fail,

> yet the unrighteous know no shame. (Zephaniah 3:5, NIV)

While this verse in Zephaniah is talking about God's chosen city, Jerusalem, it's not a stretch to apply it to us, because we are His chosen dwelling place here on earth. If we have welcomed Jesus in, shown Him spiritual hospitality by opening the door when He knocked, the Holy Spirit has come in and remains in our company.

We can recline within now and one day will rise with Jesus when He returns, knowing that nothing can separate us from the love of the Father for His children (see Romans 8:38–39).

BABY STEPS

In the past, a bully has taunted me as I fumble with soul rest: "You're not doing it right. When will you ever learn? What's wrong with you?" But that voice is not the voice of the Father. It's my voice, scolding myself for not being flawless (and yes, Satan likes to hiss accusations in my ear too).

Salvation for our souls happens right away as we admit, believe, and receive what has been done for us by Jesus Christ. But walking out the reality of soul rest is something we get better at over time as we learn more about our Father and more fully understand what is true of us because of Him.

A wise friend of mine, Jan, encourages me to speak gently to myself as I learn to walk in grace and freedom—not to self-edit but to kindly coax as I learn to rise as a daughter. As babies learn to walk, we don't get exasperated with them in the process. We offer cheers and encouragement as they become proficient walkers. We give them room and opportunities to practice. I think that's how God views our resting attempts too.

Jan assures me that I'm okay and safe as I learn to toddle in the Promised Land of grace. And that's just what this modern Martha needs to hear: that I'm going to be fine as I navigate this unpredictable, wild field of freedom.

YOU'RE IN!

I used to be the self-proclaimed president of a club in first grade. Basically, I tried to boss my friends around by setting the agenda for our playdates. I themed crafts and activities and charged a quarter for dues. It didn't go over so well.

Now I'm a loyal member of Martha's fan club, but I promise I won't dictate how you should spend your time, nor will I police your activities (but if you need a theme for your party, I'm your gal). There's already a president in charge of this group of vivacious women, and He is the wisest, kindest, most capable overseer. He shows you the way to go and outlines the work He has ordained for you to accomplish. He delights in your company. He smiles as you work as a response to being adored by Him, not in an effort to gain approval. (P.S. He already took care of the dues, for life.)

You don't lose your position as a doer daughter based on how much or little you do. You aren't more or less popular based on your abilities or the length of your to-do list. Your qualifications are based solely on His residing within.

THE BOSS'S WAY

As a girl, Tina (not her real name) never dreamed that she would one day ride in a motorcade with lights blaring and a security team with guns escorting her to the lighting of the White House Christmas tree. Tina worked as an assistant to a prominent government official, and some of her responsibilities included coordinating the scheduling team and security detail, coordinating all events and travel with her boss's wife, handling her boss's personal affairs, and doing whatever was asked of her. Since 1999 Tina's job was 24/7. She didn't necessarily work around the clock, but she was available to her boss when needed. In an average week, she worked ten-to-twelve-hour days and some block of time on weekends. Like most of the people Tina worked with, she worked until the task was done.

Successfully handling her demanding work was dependent on Tina's ability to keep a hundred balls in the air at all times. She admits that sometimes she failed, but for the most part, she managed to keep things on track. Sometimes she woke up at night realizing she'd forgotten something and made notes so that she'd remember in the morning. I don't know about you, but hearing about Tina's responsibilities induces stress (yet sounds exhilarating too)! I am curious about Tina's secret for excelling in this high-pressure job, besides her being a strong and capable woman. The secret isn't found in an energy drink or a regimen of expensive vitamins; it is closely related to who she worked for and the kind of boss he was.

According to Tina, her boss and his wife are two of the kindest people she knows. Although he didn't have to, her boss included Tina and her husband in amazing events in DC, strictly out of kindness. She went to the White House more times than she can count. At a private Embassy party years ago, he made a point to call Tina over and introduce her to the president's wife. The deepest joy for Tina was knowing that her boss counted on her, trusted her, and respected her. He genuinely appreciated everything she did for him and expressed that, even when she made mistakes.

What strikes me about Tina is the way she willingly inconvenienced herself and served faithfully for the greater good. This says a lot about her character and her boss too.

When we discover the true character of God, it becomes a joy to serve Him, because we know we are valued by a kind Father. Sure, there are times carrying out His instructions is inconvenient and difficult, yet we know we can trust Him. And even when we fail, His grace buoys us. We've been given so much and are compelled to give back, not just to avoid consequences but because we want to honor the One who is worthy.

We remember that the All-Sufficient One is on the throne of heaven and lives in us. He freely extends undeserved grace, and we would be fools not to favorably respond. We take care of what's given because we realize how expensive it was: scourged flesh, punctured feet, thorn-crown-pierced temples. We offer the gift of grace to others because we are overwhelmed with gratitude by what has been selflessly provided.

We bow our knees, admitting our need. We receive the Bread of heaven, broken for us, able to satisfy continuously. We stand, knowing that our Father has not held out on us. Through love, personified in Jesus, He brings us home.

We enjoy what's ours, like carefree girls running through the sprinkler on a sweltering day, oblivious to body-image issues and refusing to withhold our total delight. We experience freedom as we work, play, and rest as daughters, assured of the kindness of our Dad.

DEFINING THE CULTURE

Some friends of ours define their family's culture by their name and the positive characteristics they want to be known for. For example, if one of their kids lies, they say, "We are Martins, and Martins don't lie." Or if they want to model or point out a positive behavior, they might say, "We are Martins, and Martins are generous to others."

We use a similar strategy with our kids. And we tell them, "I love you, no matter what." We want our kids to know that even though they mess up, their place in our family is secure. We may not like their behavior at times (nor they ours), but we are committed to loving them. That doesn't mean we condone sinful behavior or make excuses for their wrongdoing, but their position is settled; they are family, for life.

For years, Marthas have been characterized by negative attributes, such as worrying, not being present in the moment, and having a my-way-or-the-highway mentality. But let's change the culture, shall we? Let's be known for receiving and extending grace to others (and ourselves) as we get things done:

- We are Marthas, and Marthas are beloved daughters who serve from a place of strength and peace.
- We are Marthas, and Marthas are designed to do great things for God and freed to rest in His greatness.
- We are Marthas, and Marthas are dependable and dependent on the One who has done it all.
- We are Marthas, and Marthas are loved no matter what, even when we get it wrong, fall short, or fail.

You don't have to worship, then work; you can worship as you work. May you view your God-given wiring as a catalyst in working for the Lord, not as an obstacle blocking the way.

These characteristics of our family culture define us as we grow, by the help of the Holy Spirit. We agree with what's already true and believe that He will develop and produce fruit in us.

We ask Dad to help us live out what defines us as daughters. He responds that a daughter

- is a good steward of what she has been given (1 Corinthians 4:2)
- goes to God for rest when weary (Matthew 11:28–29)
- rests in her position as God's daughter (John 10:27–29)

- trusts in God (Proverbs 3:5; Isaiah 26:3)
- casts worries on Him (Psalm 55:22; 1 Peter 5:7)
- acknowledges Him as Lord (Proverbs 3:6)
- prays when anxious and tells Him her requests (Philippians 4:6)
- doesn't worry about what she will eat, drink, or wear (Matthew 6:25)
- works as for the Lord (Colossians 3:23)
- perseveres when faced with trials (James 1:2)
- worships the Lord with gladness (Psalm 100:2)
- lives by faith (Galatians 2:20)
- loves Jesus and gives Him her best (Deuteronomy 10:12)
- is created in Christ Jesus to do good works but realizes she is not saved through works (Ephesians 2:8–10)

And we remember what characterizes our Dad. Our Father

- sustains all creation, including us (Job 12:10)
- provides rest for souls (Matthew 11:28–30)
- never sleeps (Psalm 121:4)
- keeps in perfect peace those whose minds are steadfast (Isaiah 26:3)
- sustains us and helps us (Psalm 54:4)
- will watch over us, cover us, and direct us (Psalm 121:5–8; Proverbs 3:6)
- will guard our hearts and minds through His peace (Philippians 4:7)
- takes care of our needs and feeds and clothes us (Matthew 6:26, 30)
- fulfills His good purpose in us (Philippians 2:13)
- is our refuge and strength and very present help in trouble (Psalm 46:1)

- sent His Son to serve, not to be served (Mark 10:45)
- created everything and is worthy of worship (Revelation 4:11)
- is pleased by our faith (Hebrews 11:6)
- loves us and gave His Son for us (John 3:16)
- sent Jesus to faithfully finish the work we could not do ourselves (John 17:2–4)

Modern Martha **Dalene Reyburn**

When we remember that we're daughters first and doers second, then our doings aren't done out of pride or desperate insecurity. We don't panic. We begin to lean hard into our passions, gifts, and opportunities, trusting God to position us in ways that best reflect Him. We maximize the days left to us by doing what we can with what we have in the time we have in the place we are, out of joy and freedom from law. We begin doing with even greater enthusiasm and much greater love because there's a sure and quiet knowing that already, Jesus has done it all.[2]

☐ **It Is Finished:** The Certificate of Ownership

Personalize the certificate on the next page to remind you of who you are and what is already yours in Christ. (A downloadable copy is available at www .katiemreid.com/martha-resources.)

CERTIFICATE OF OWNERSHIP

_____

Date of Issue

This is to serve as a reminder to

_____

(Fill in your full name)

that her redemption has been fully paid by Jesus Christ
at the cost of His pure and precious blood through
His completed work on the cross.

By faith, _____ has believed
and received what has been accomplished on her behalf
through the death, burial, and resurrection of Christ.

Through Christ's work, she is a new creation
and has been freed from a life of slavery.

Through her adoption, _____ now
has access to all rights and privileges given by her Father,
because she is His daughter, now and forever.

10

Dear Modern Martha

Serving from a Place of Strength and Peace

ᔧ

> This resurrection life you received from God is not a
> timid, grave-tending life. It's adventurously expectant,
> greeting God with a childlike "What's next, Papa?"
> God's Spirit touches our spirits and confirms who we
> really are. We know who he is, and we know who we
> are: Father and children. And we know we are going to
> get what's coming to us—an unbelievable inheritance!
> We go through exactly what Christ goes through. If we
> go through the hard times with him, then we're cer-
> tainly going to go through the good times with him!
>
> **—Romans 8:15–17, MSG**

*J*esus *loved* Martha. Somehow I overlooked that fact. Jesus wasn't re-
jecting her; He was addressing her spiritual posture as she served. He
wasn't telling Martha to stop being who He designed her to be; He was
pointing out that she did not have to work herself into a frenzy to be loved.

Jesus knowingly invited her to exchange worry for worship and to exchange a frantic state of mind for a settled soul. Martha was already adored by Jesus, and His love was a gift to be received, not a prize to be earned.

Mary was literally sitting at Jesus's feet, but Martha was invited to sit figuratively with Him even while she hosted and to rest in who she already was: loved, treasured, and smiled on, regardless of how the meal turned out. Jesus was asking Martha to trust Him, even if the outcome looked different than she expected. He was tenderly pointing her to the fact that I AM was present in her home. He was unveiling hope to come.

Jesus was inviting Martha to find soul rest amid her serving. He wasn't asking her to hang up her apron but rather to resign her efforts to earn what already belonged to her. Her to-do list had value, but it did not determine her value. What Martha didn't yet know was that she could sit down once and for all, from a spiritual standpoint, because Jesus was going to complete the greatest to-do list of all time.

Jesus interrupted Martha with love, as Banner did when he came to my side of the bed in the middle of the night to offer me a hug. And I don't want to miss it next time. I don't want to miss Him amid my doing.

When my son showed up in the wee hours, I assumed he needed something from me. And I was so exhausted from trying to be enough that I had nothing left to give. I missed out on receiving his affection because my earning and proving mentality had robbed me of receiving God's unconditional love.

The constant tension between doing and being, coupled with the reprimands poor Martha has received through the ages, led me to assume there was something wrong with being a doer. Until I woke up. Like having a blindfold removed, the dust settled and I saw Martha, fellow doers, and eventually myself from a different perspective.

Jesus didn't ask Martha to stop being a doer. And He doesn't ask us to be someone else to be accepted. We are created to be doers and that's a good thing indeed. We don't have to apologize anymore for being modern Marthas. *She's fantastic, and so are you!*

If you have invited Christ into the home of your heart, if you have welcomed Him in as Savior and received His completed work on the cross, then He has taken up residence within you. Jesus, Emmanuel ("God with us"), dwells *within*, and you don't have to keep cleaning your house, or your heart, to keep Him there.

You are just as close to God when you're sitting quietly as when you are scrubbing vigorously. Why? Because Jesus's love has already been proved. So we can stop trying to prove ourselves, whether through sitting at His feet or through serving. Sitting and serving are both necessary, but not to achieve the approval that already has been given through Christ.

Freedom can be found in the "do" because Jesus already did that for which we are striving.

The scolding is silenced as we tune into tenderness. The static dissolves as hope crescendos. The royal banner of Love waves overhead, over heart, like a seal depicting ownership. We receive the invitation to come as we are: open handed, with nothing required but belief.

The big to-do has already been done.

Perfection. *Check.*

Salvation. *Check.*

Restoration. *Check.*

We are invited to take a break from our to-do lists as we uncover the big to-do of His extravagant grace. Grace is a game changer. It changes everything. Grace answers the question of our lack, our sin, our striving, and our identity with Enough.

You are made like Martha because God saw fit to create you that way. He has gone to great lengths to demonstrate how devoted He is to you.

Jesus loves *you*—even when you are short fused, whether or not you have a quiet time, and even in the midst of tackling your to-do list.

Let's stop discounting our God-given design. Let's discover the secret to living seated within as our works express gratitude for what is ours in Christ. Then let's rise and walk in newfound freedom as we embrace a love that doesn't turn away.

May these words give way to fresh revelation of timeless truth. May worry turn to worship and may striving turn to settledness as we receive the One who wove us wonderfully together, just as He did with Martha.

FREEDOM CALLS

Friend, in case there's any doubt, I think you're fabulous! The way you take on projects, manage people, and help others warms my heart. You think things through and are a good problem solver. I smile as I watch you do your thing and get things done.

You embrace your design as a doer and enjoy your position as a daughter as you go forward in faith. And by the way, props for finishing this book. Go check it off your to-do list. But before you tackle the next item, I want to tell you about one more doer daughter.

You may already know her—I hope. Her given name was Araminta "Minty" Ross, and she was a slave in the South. In her late twenties, she escaped to freedom and adopted the name Harriet Tubman. Harriet battled against the reality of her personal slavery by bravely making her way to the metaphorical Promised Land in the North: "When I found I had crossed dat line, I looked at my hands to see if I was de same pusson. There was such a glory ober ebery ting; de sun came like gold through the trees, and ober the fields, and I felt like I was in Heaben."[1]

It would have been understandable for Harriet to remain in the place where slaves were free and make a life for herself there, yet she chose to risk her life and return to slave territory so that others (nearly three hundred) could be led to freedom. Harriet earned the nickname Moses for her role as conductor on the Underground Railroad. She was free but chose to use her freedom to go back and lead others out of bondage. The threat of dogs, hunger, injury, bullets, capture, and even death did not deter Harriet from being a willing vessel to liberate her people.[2]

Are you willing to do the same?

Through the good news of grace, you have moved from the hired-help mentality to the reality of a beloved daughter. You have thrown off worry, guilt, and your attempts to carry the weight of the world on your shoulders. You now rest within, knowing that, even in trials, you are not alone. You are convinced of the good Father's love for you and are ready to work as a response to that love—from a place of peace.

It would be easy to go about your business, enjoying grace and newfound freedom. But I'll bet that if you slow just for a moment, you can hear them— your fellow sisters—straining, stressing, and maybe even calling out for help. They may be in your family, at the office, down the street, or across the seas. Maybe they have never heard the good news, maybe they've forgotten what's so good about it, or maybe they are camped out in the trenches of slave territory, never realizing that the battle has already been won.

But you know the truth. You have seen the light. You are unchained.

Will you, as a freed woman, help show them the way home?

Modern Martha · Christy Mobley

I can get caught up in my own legalism and forget that I'm covered with grace and have freedom in Christ. I just plain forget it. I forget that's who I am and what I have. Because I am driven to please God, I try to do everything He says more because of a law thing than a love thing. And I have to go back and read Galatians and remind myself that I am free: "It is for freedom that Christ has set us free. Stand firm, then, and do not let yourselves be burdened again by a yoke of slavery" (5:1, NIV). And it takes the anxiety away, and it's like "Oh, I forgot—I'm free. I obey God because I love Him, not because I have to. I'm free to choose to obey Him."³

☐ **It Is Finished:** Beloved Daughter's Decree

Read the Beloved Daughter's Decree on the following page. Visit www .katiemreid.com/martha-resources for a download of the decree.

The Beloved Daughter's Decree

1. **I am loved.**
   Jesus's love has already been proven, so I can stop trying to prove myself.

2. **I am secure.**
   God is more powerful than my worries and worthy of my worship.

3. **I am cared for.**
   Jesus is more than able to shoulder what I carry and hold me close when I fall.

4. **My redemption is paid by Jesus's blood.**
   I don't have to strive for what I already have.

5. **I am a recipient of grace.**
   Grace is a gift I receive, not a prize I earn.

6. **I possess a delightful inheritance.**
   Freedom is mine because Christ has delivered me from slavery.

7. **I am enough because Jesus is enough.**
   Perfection is not up to me; it is in me, and His name is Jesus.

8. **I choose to rest in Christ's sufficiency.**
   God is working even when I am not.

9. **I follow God's loving lead.**
   Assured of the kindness of my Dad, I work, play, and rest as a beloved daughter.

10. **I am made like Martha.**
    I am freed from a life of striving and now serve from a place of peace.

Bible Study

The Enemy of your soul certainly doesn't want you to walk in spiritual freedom or help others do so. So how do you remain grounded in the fertile soil of grace and let the roots of truth grow deep and strong? I believe that it is by knowing the truth and letting the truth set (and keep) you free. Through the following *Made Like Martha* Bible study, discover how to navigate your busy life in light of the good news that has been unearthed. This isn't just more to do; this study has been carefully designed to solidify key scriptures so you can walk confidently as a beloved daughter, day in and day out.

$\mathcal{W}$elcome to the *Made Like Martha* Bible study! May God's Word ground you in hope as you take a closer look at the biblical principles addressed in this book. Gain a better understanding of the good news that is yours in Christ by utilizing five powerful study tools: (1) marking key words, (2) making lists, (3) studying action words, (4) looking up Greek definitions, and (5) cross-referencing. Each week a new inductive study tool is presented. Try each of them to discover which is your favorite (mine is making lists—go figure!). The inductive approach is geared toward us doers, because we study the Bible systematically and purposefully.

There is a lot of rich content here (for those of you who have the word *overachiever* tattooed on your ankle), but do as much or as little as you'd like. If you just read the key scripture each week, great! Celebrate that! There is so much grace as you interact with this study. Do what works for you.

There are five lessons in the Bible study and ten chapters in the *Made Like Martha* book. Each lesson corresponds with key concepts found within two chapters of the book. You can read the book before, during, or after this study—whichever works best for you. Each lesson focuses on two key passages from the Bible. There is a spot for you to add a check mark after you finish each component. You can complete each lesson in a week or break it up over two weeks. Go at your own pace as you mine timeless truths from Scripture. The goal is to know more of God's Word than when you started.

There are four main steps that we will be using for each lesson in this study, which can be remembered using the acronym WORD:

Worship: This first step includes the prep work for your week of study. You'll find the key Scripture passages and space to practice learning the key Scripture verse. Pray and thank God for His Word. Ask Him to illuminate what He wants you to learn, and then read the passage and write the key scriptures.

Observe: This second step includes instructions for the featured inductive-Bible-study tool and then gives you the opportunity to try it out. Reread the passage slowly, and then go back and use the inductive study tool of the week to dig in deeper the second time you read it.

Reflect: This third step includes the "Heart Work" section, with questions about the key passages, and the "Soul Care" section, with personal questions about the lesson's topic. Think about what you have learned from Scripture and how it affects you personally by working through these sections.

Do!: This fourth step gives you a five-minute exercise to apply what you have learned. Don't just hear the Word; go and "do what it says" (James 1:22, NIV).

Before we get started, here are a couple of helpful hints:

If you're doing the Bible Study as a group gathering: Use the individual study as the homework for your group study, and the group questions and activity for your meeting time together. The group study is set up for five weeks, but you could also choose to meet every other week (for ten weeks) so that participants have more time to complete each lesson. Or the group study can stand alone (without the individual study). If you prefer to simplify it this way, group members could read the lesson's key Scripture passages and practice learning the key verses in preparation for the group gathering. If you do a group study, email katie@katiemreid.com and let me know so I can pray for you and maybe even surprise your group with a video appearance, if time allows.

If you're the group leader: There is a section just for you, to help you prepare as you lead. The group activities are designed to help your group embrace their wiring as doers and engage both their minds and their hands. Use what works for your group or adjust as needed.

If you'd like to be part of an online community: Connect with other modern Marthas as you interact with God's Word and encourage one another. Join the fun by adding #MadeLikeMartha to your social-media posts. We'd love to see a picture of you with the book, working on your study, or with your group.

Are you ready to get started? Great! Gather these supplies so we can dig in: a Bible, your *Made Like Martha* book, and colored pencils or pens. If you are not comfortable marking up your Bible, you can print the Scripture passages for each lesson from www.biblegateway.com. You might also want to use a journal if you prefer to answer the questions and do the activities there instead.

Let's grow in grace and depth of insight, together.

Dear Father,

Thank You for the woman holding this study—the one You have lovingly created. Encourage her heart and strengthen her soul as she learns more about Your goodness. May she receive Your affection and marvel at Your power as she discovers more of You in the Bible. In a world where people seem to believe whatever sounds right to them, reveal Your timeless, dependable truth that she can stand on no matter what. May this study serve as a tool to help her accurately handle Your Word as she walks by faith, knowing how deeply she is loved by You.

In Jesus's name, amen.

Sample Group Gathering Time:

- Welcome the group and make announcements.
- Lead group members in getting to know one another. (Example: Have each person share her name, her favorite and least favorite things to do around the house or at work, and one thing she is looking forward to about this study.)
- Open in prayer.
- Remind the group of key points from the lesson.
- Facilitate group discussion based on the questions provided or come up with your own.
- Lead the group activity (before, during, or after you go through the group discussion questions).
- Close in prayer.
- Remind the group of any pertinent information for the next time you gather.

Lesson

☑ 1

A Loved Heart, a Worshipful Soul

We know that for those who love God all things work together for good, for those who are called according to his purpose.

—Romans 8:28

> **Book Chapters:** This lesson coordinates with chapters 1 and 2.
>
> **Key Passages:** Romans 8 and Revelation 4:8–11
>
> **Key Scripture:** Romans 8:28
>
> **Inductive Study Tool:** Marking key words
>
> **Lesson 1 Instructions:** Answer the questions and check off each
> step after you complete it.

I. WORSHIP

Thank God for who He is and ask Him to illuminate what He wants to show
you about His Word through this lesson.

_____ Read Romans 8 and Revelation 4:8–11.

_____ Write Romans 8:28 in the space below or in your journal,
or design an image online.

II. OBSERVE

This week we are marking key words to quickly learn more about God the
Father, Jesus the Son, and the Holy Spirit our Helper. (We will expand on this
exercise in lesson 2.) Grab your favorite pens or colored pencils and choose a
simple symbol to write on top of each person of the Trinity and the corre-
sponding pronouns in Romans 8. (Remember, you can print out Romans 8
from www.biblegateway.com if you don't want to mark up your Bible.) For
example, you could draw a triangle for God, a cross for Jesus, and a circle for

the Holy Spirit. For consistency, consider using the same color for all members of the Trinity. Also mark the word *love* (with a red heart) in this chapter.

The law of the Spirit of life has set you free in Christ Jesus from the law of sin and death. (Romans 8:2)

_____ Reread Romans 8 and mark key words (*God, Jesus, Spirit,* and *love*).

III. REFLECT

Heart Work
_____ Answer the following questions based on what you read and marked in the key passages.

Questions for Romans 8

1. What is one verse that stood out to you, and why?

2. What did you learn by marking the word *love*?

3. According to Romans 8, what are some things that are true of those who are in Christ Jesus? (For example, verse 1 says, "There is . . . no condemnation for those who are in Christ Jesus.")

Questions for Revelation 4:8–11

4. The word *throne* is used three times in this passage. Record all you learn from observing this word in these verses. (For example, Revelation 4:9 reveals that the one who sits on the throne receives glory, honor, and thanks and lives forever and ever.)

5. According to Revelation 4:11, why is God worthy?

Soul Care

_____ Answer the following questions as you reflect on this week's passages.

6. Recall a time you felt really loved by someone else. What were the circumstances surrounding that experience?

7. Is there something keeping you from believing you are loved by God? How can you address those feelings with the truth found in Romans 8:31–39?

8. Write down a specific worry that you have.

9. Now choose a verse from Romans 8 or Revelation 4:8–11 (or elsewhere in the Bible) that helps combat this worry with the truth. Write the verse here.

IV. DO!

_____ Worship can help us starve worry. Take several minutes to worship God in your favorite way. For example, draw, go for a quick walk or run, sing, dance, or read a psalm. Whatever you choose to do, connect with God while you do it.

_____ Tell a friend what you learned or share the key scripture with him or her. Share a photo of your key scripture on social media and tag it with #MadeLikeMartha, or visit www.katiemreid.com /martha-resources to access free images.

_____ Well done! You completed lesson 1! Now rest in a way that is meaningful to you.

Group Gathering

Instructions for Leaders

Pray: Pray that God would help your group realize the depth of His love for each of them and His ability to take care of them.

Prep: Have 3 x 5 index cards (or sticky notes) and pens available for each member of your group for activity 1 described on the next page. Decide whether you would like to pray over worries as a group or have each person pass her worry to the person next to her. Decide whether you are going to go out to eat, host a meal, or cook a meal together as a group for activity 2. Communicate pertinent information to group members ahead of time.

Activities

1. Have each person write down a worry she has on a small piece of paper. Someone could collect the worries in a container and then pull them out and pray over each one, or everyone could pass the worry to the person next to her, who will then pray for that concern for the week.

2. Go out to eat as a group, host a meal for the group at your house, or plan to cook a meal together at the end of your gathering time or even while you are discussing questions 1–4. The point of the meal element is to help you remember to feast on worship and starve worry. If you cook a meal together, make a double portion and arrange to take a meal (or a gift card) to someone in your church or community who is facing a worrisome situation.

Key Points

- Nothing can separate us from God's love, not even our to-do lists.
- We starve worry when we feast on worship.

Group Discussion

1. What verse in Romans 8 gives you the most hope? What was a verse in that chapter that challenged you?

2. Share the key scripture (Romans 8:28) from memory if you'd like and/or share an image if you designed one (no guilt here, only grace!).

3. What is your favorite way to worship God? What is an obstacle you face in worshipping Him?

4. If you are comfortable, share your answers from questions 8 and 9 of the individual study (What is a worry that you have, and what is one truth that helps you combat that worry?).

5. Share with the group something that stood out to you from chapter 1 or 2 of the book.

Lesson

☑ 2

A Daughter's Heart, a Redeemed Soul

You are no longer a slave, but a [daughter], and
if a [daughter], then an heir through God.

—Galatians 4:7

I. WORSHIP

Thank God for who He is and ask Him to illuminate what He wants to show
you about His Word through this lesson.

_____ Read Galatians 4:1–7 and Hebrews 9.

_____ Write Galatians 4:7 in the space below or in your journal,
or design an image online.

II. OBSERVE

This week we are making a list (my favorite tool!) so we can learn powerful
truths about God the Father, Jesus the Son, and the Holy Spirit our Helper.
First, mark key words as you did in the previous lesson, for both passages.
After you have done that, choose God, Jesus, or the Holy Spirit and make a
list of everything you learned about Him from the text. Include the reference
of where you found it. Start with where your first key word is found for that
person of the Trinity. Don't add to what the text says; let the Word speak

for itself. This is a simple yet transformative tool. If you're up for it, go back and make a list for the other two members of the Trinity also. Keep these lists handy and add to them as you read other passages. If you're really ambitious, go back to week 1 and make lists out of your key words from those verses too.

Example list for *God* in Galatians 4:

- God sent His Son to redeem those under the law so we might receive adoption (verses 4–5).
- God has sent the Spirit of His Son into our hearts because we are His children (verse 6).
- God has heirs—His children (verse 7).

_____ Reread Galatians 4:1–7 and mark key words (*God, Jesus, Holy Spirit**). Then choose one of these key words and make a list of all you learned about that member of the Trinity in this passage (include references, see example above). *Jesus is referred to as "Son" and the Holy Spirit as "Spirit of his Son" in these verses, so mark accordingly, using the same symbols that you used for these in lesson 1.

_____ Reread Hebrews 9 and mark key words (*Christ, covenant, blood*). Then choose one of these key words and make a list of all you learned about it (include references).

III. REFLECT

Heart Work

____ Answer the following questions based on what you read and
marked in the key passages.

Questions for Galatians 4:1–7

1. What is one thing you learned about slaves through this passage?

2. What is one thing you learned about being an heir in this passage?

3. Are you a slave to sin or an adopted daughter of God? How do you
know?

Questions for Hebrews 9

4. According to Hebrews 9, what are three ways the first covenant and
new covenant are similar?

5. What are three ways the first covenant and the new covenant differ?

6. Reread Hebrews 9:18–22. What is required for the forgiveness of sins?

7. Write a prayer of thanksgiving in light of God being your Father and you being His daughter. If you are unsure whether you are God's daughter, visit the "It Is Finished" section on page 69 to see what is required to become His.

Soul Care

_____ Answer the following questions as you reflect on this week's passages.

8. Do you tend to live as a slave of God or as His daughter? Why do you think this is?

9. In light of what you have learned about Father God and being His daughter, what is something you have believed about Him that is not true? (For example: "After I was saved, I lived as if I had to make up for my sin through good works.")

10. What is a truth that can help counter the lie you have believed (see question 9)? (For example: "Hebrews 9:14 reveals that Jesus's blood is what cleanses our conscience from dead works.")

IV. Do!

_____ Take five minutes and turn your Trinity list into a prayer by thanking God, Jesus, or the Holy Spirit for each of His attributes and abilities revealed in these passages.

_____ Tell a friend what you learned or share the key scripture with him or her. Share a photo of your key scripture on social media and tag it with #MadeLikeMartha, or visit www.katiemreid.com /martha-resources to access free images.

_____ Well done! You completed lesson 2! Now rest in a way that is meaningful to you.

Group Gathering

Instructions for Leaders

Pray: Pray that God would help your group understand the Father's heart toward them and the riches of His grace available in Christ. Be mindful of those who have lost their fathers, are estranged from them, or have wounds from them. This could be a hard yet healing week for them.

Prep: Gather the necessary supplies for the activity you choose (see next paragraph). Communicate to your group what they need to bring with them and where you will be meeting this week (if it changes based on the activity you choose).

Activity: Revisit the list of daughter activities found in chapter 3 on pages 47–48 for an idea for this week's activity. Choose one or a few of them (or come up with your own) to do as a group. Maybe go to a park and swing, bring some flowers to your gathering and make flower wreaths, or have a coloring-book party. The point is to let loose and have fun and enjoy the carefree spirit of daughters who trust their good Father. Discuss the questions for this week before, after, or during your activity (whichever works best for your group).

Key Points
- We are adopted as God's children and are no longer slaves to sin.
- Admit you're a sinner, believe in Jesus's sacrifice for sin, and claim Him as your Savior.

Group Discussion
1. What verse in Galatians 4 communicated good news to you?

2. Share the key scripture (Galatians 4:7) from memory if you'd like and/or share an image if you designed one (no guilt here, only grace!).

3. According to Hebrews 9:11–12, by what means did Christ enter the holy places, and how many times?

4. If you are comfortable, share about whether you live more like a slave or a daughter (question 8 of the individual study).

5. Share with the group something that stood out to you from chapter 3 or 4 of the book.

Lesson

☑ 3

A Grace-Filled Heart, a Secure Soul

In him we have redemption through his blood, the forgiveness of our trespasses, according to the riches of his grace, which he lavished upon us, in all wisdom and insight.

—Ephesians 1:7–8

I. WORSHIP

Thank God for who He is and ask Him to illuminate what He wants to show you about His Word through this lesson.

_____ Read Ephesians 1 and 1 Peter 1:3–13.

_____ Write Ephesians 1:7–8 in the space below or in your journal, or design an image online.

II. OBSERVE

This week we are going to take a closer look at the action words (verbs) in the key passages. Doing so will help us dig deeper into the text and explore the benefits of belonging to Christ.

_____ Reread Ephesians 1 and underline all the action words that any member of the Trinity does. For example: "God has blessed us with every spiritual blessing" (verse 3).

_____ Reread 1 Peter 1:3–13 and underline the action words in verses 8–13 that we, as believers, are to do. For example: "<u>Love</u> him" (verse 8) and "<u>Believe</u> in him" (verse 8).

III. REFLECT

Heart Work

_____ Answer the following questions based on what you read and marked in the key passages.

Questions for Ephesians 1

1. What is one of your favorite attributes of God, Jesus, or the Holy Spirit from Ephesians 1? Why?

2. Reread Ephesians 1:15–19. Paul prays that the eyes of your heart would be enlightened so "that you may know what is _____ _____, what are the _____ _____, and what is the _____."

Questions for 1 Peter 1:3–13

3. What do you learn about hope in 1 Peter 1:3?

4. In 1 Peter 1:4–5, what words describe the spiritual inheritance of believers?

5. In light of 1 Peter 1:6–7, what is a benefit of trials?

Soul Care

_____ Answer the following questions as you reflect on this week's passages.

6. Is it difficult for you to enjoy the benefits of grace through Christ's sacrifice? If so, why do you think that is?

7. Recall a time you were shown grace by someone or showed it to someone else. How did you feel afterward?

8. Are you secure in your salvation, or do you feel as though you can lose it?

9. Ask God to guide you as you look for a verse or two in Ephesians 1 and 1 Peter 1:3–13 to support your stance in question 8.

IV. Do!

_____ Take five minutes and listen to (or sing) a song that talks about the grace of Jesus. There are some great hymns and worship songs to choose from. Or if you feel inspired, write your own song or poem about grace.

_____ Tell a friend what you learned or share the key scripture with him or her. Share a photo of your key scripture on social media and tag it with #MadeLikeMartha, or visit www.katiemreid.com /martha-resources to access free images.

_____ Well done! You completed lesson 3! Now rest in a way that is meaningful to you.

Group Gathering

Instructions for Leaders

Pray: Pray that God would help your group open up and share their hearts this week. Pray for any in your group who don't know the Lord as Savior to be drawn to Him and receive Him.

Prep: Gather the necessary supplies for the encouragement-card activity. Decide whether you will purchase the supplies or whether you want each person to bring supplies with her. Decide ahead of time who will be receiving the cards. Feel free to ask the group to help you come up with a list of recipients. Bring stamps and addresses if the cards are going to be mailed.

Activity: As a group, write encouragement cards to someone who is sick, shut in, or struggling. Pray that God will use the letters to bring hope to the hurting. Mail the letters or hand deliver one (or all) of them if time allows. As usual, discuss the group questions before, during, or after the activity.

Key Points
- God has lavished the gift of grace on those who belong to Him.
- You don't have to strive for what you already have in Christ.

Group Discussion
1. What is a spiritual blessing that you are currently enjoying?

2. Share the key scripture (Ephesians 1:7–8) from memory if you'd like and/or share an image if you designed one (no guilt here, only grace!).

3. If you are comfortable, share a trial you are currently facing.

4. What is a truth from 1 Peter 1:3–13 that brings you hope in light of this trial?

5. Share with the group something that stood out to you from chapter 5 or 6 of the book.

Lesson

☑ 4

A Hopeful Heart,
a Peaceful Soul

For freedom Christ has set us free; stand firm therefore, and do not submit again to a yoke of slavery.

—Galatians 5:1

I. WORSHIP

Thank God for who He is and ask Him to illuminate what He wants to show
you about His Word through this lesson.

_____ Read Galatians 5 and Hebrews 4:9–16.

_____ Write Galatians 5:1 in the space below or in your journal,
or design an image online.

II. OBSERVE

This week we are going to learn how to look up definitions of words in the
language in which they were originally written—Greek—as these passages
are from the New Testament. (Hebrew is the original language of the Old
Testament.) It is important to use a word-for-word translation when looking
up the original language, which is why we are using ESV.

Go to www.blueletterbible.org, type "Galatians 5:1" in the search bar,
and select ESV for the version. Click on the blue "Tools" bar to the left of the

verse. Find the word you want to look up (in this case *freedom*) and click on the Strong's number. You will see a *G* (for "Greek") before the Strong's number. *Freedom* is G1657. Click on that number. A new screen will come up with the Greek word, pronunciation, and definition (among other things). Access the dictionary aids and see the biblical usage to help you gain more understanding about what *freedom* means in Galatians 5:1.

Example: *freedom* (G1657, *eleutheria*). If we click on the *Vine's Expository Dictionary* entry, we learn that freedom (or liberty) in Galatians 5:1 emphasizes "the completeness of the act"—that "it was done once for all."

The "Outline of Biblical Usage" section says that *freedom* in this verse refers to "liberty to do or to omit things having no relationship to salvation." Hint: If you got stuck on the first few steps of this study tool, use this link to access the direct definition page for *freedom:* www.blueletterbible.org/lang /lexicon/lexicon.cfm?Strongs=G1657&t=ESV.

_____ Reread Galatians 5 and then look up the Greek word for "Spirit" in Galatians 5 using www.blueletterbible.org (or a Strong's concordance for ESV). Be sure to use context when trying to decide which definition best fits the passage. For example, we can safely deduce that *Spirit* is not referring to a human spirit in this passage. Record your findings here.

III. REFLECT

Heart Work

_____ Answer the following questions based on what you read and marked in the key passages.

Questions for Galatians 5

1. What are three things you learned about the Spirit from Galatians 5?

2. According to Galatians 5:13, what are we to use our freedom for?

3. What are three things to avoid in our relationships with others (see Galatians 5:26)?

Questions for Hebrews 4:9–16

4. What did you learn about the word *rest* from reading Hebrews 4:9–11?

5. On the following page, read the note about Sabbath rest. This helps us understand that Sabbath rest is not referring to an obligatory weekly day of rest in these particular verses but a restful state of Christ at home in us and also us at home with Him now and then fully in eternity. What do these verses tell us about why we can rest?

Note: Via www.blueletterbible.org, *Vine's Expository Dictionary* gives this explanation for *Sabbath rest* (found in Hebrews 4:9): "Here the sabbath-keeping is the perpetual sabbath 'rest' to be enjoyed uninterruptedly by believers in their fellowship with the Father and the Son, in contrast to the weekly Sabbath under the Law. Because this sabbath 'rest' is the 'rest' of God Himself, Hbr 4:10, its full fruition is yet future, though believers now enter into it. In whatever way they enter into Divine 'rest,' that which they enjoy is involved in an indissoluble relation with God."[1]

Soul Care

_____ Answer the following questions as you reflect on this week's passages.

6. What is one of your biggest barriers to rest (physically, emotionally, and spiritually)?

7. Do your actions communicate that you are living in the freedom that comes from Christ or under the yoke of slavery under the Law?

8. Look over the works of the flesh in Galatians 5:19–21. Are you currently struggling with one of these? Take a moment to talk to God about this issue. He is more than able to forgive you and help you take the next step to freedom from this sin.

9. If you are in Christ, then the Spirit is residing and working within you. What is one of your favorite fruits of the Spirit to see in your own life and in the lives of those around you?

IV. Do!

_____ Take five minutes and write down some things that bring you joy and peace.

_____ Tell a friend what you learned or share the key scripture with him or her. Share a photo of your key scripture on social media and tag it with #MadeLikeMartha, or visit www.katiemreid.com /martha-resources to access free images.

_____ Well done! You completed lesson 4! Now rest in a way that is meaningful to you.

Group Gathering

Instructions for Leaders

Pray: Pray that God would help your group sense His nearness in a fresh way.

Prep: Select an activity, make arrangements for it, and gather the necessary supplies. Communicate any information that your group needs to know.

Activity: Plan an activity that is relaxing for your group. Here are some ideas: invite a musician to come play a few soothing songs, have a nail-painting party, have a local artist come teach basic hand lettering (consider writing out one of the key verses), host a coffee and dessert bar. As usual, discuss the group questions before, during, or after the group activity.

Key Points

- Perfection is not up to us; it is in us, and His name is Jesus.
- We can trust God to work even when we aren't working.

Group Discussion

1. According to Galatians 5:16–26, what does walking by the Spirit look like?

2. Share the key scripture (Galatians 5:1) from memory if you'd like and/or share an image if you designed one (no guilt here, only grace!).

3. If you are comfortable, share an area where you are overdoing it or underdoing it.

4. Talk about a time God clearly directed you.

5. Share with the group something that stood out to you from chapter 7 or 8 of the book.

Lesson
☑ 5

A Settled Heart, a Freed Soul

By grace you have been saved through faith. And this is not your own doing; it is the gift of God, not a result of works, so that no one may boast. For we are his workmanship, created in Christ Jesus for good works, which God prepared beforehand, that we should walk in them.

—Ephesians 2:8–10

I. WORSHIP

Thank God for who He is and ask Him to illuminate what He wants to show
you about His Word through this lesson.

_____ Read Ephesians 2 and Romans 5.

_____ Write Ephesians 2:8–10 in the space below or in your journal,
or design an image online.

II. OBSERVE

You have learned how to mark key words, make lists, isolate action words,
and look up definitions of Greek words. Well done! Pick your favorite of
those four tools to try out again on this lesson's passages. Let's also add one
more tool during this final lesson. Cross-referencing involves looking up
verses (elsewhere in the Bible) that relate to the topic or verses at hand. It is
important to read the key passages several times to gain a better understanding before starting to cross-reference with other verses. Cross-referencing is a

simple yet powerful tool to provide breadth and depth in our understanding of Scripture. We will incorporate this tool in the "Heart Check" section.

_____ Reread Ephesians 2 and use your favorite tool from lessons 1–4 to help you observe this passage further.

_____ Reread Romans 5 and use your tool of choice from lessons 1–4 to help you understand this passage in a deeper way.

III. REFLECT

Heart Work

_____ Answer the following questions based on what you read and marked in the key passages.

Questions for Ephesians 2

1. Read Romans 3:28. What does this verse add to your understanding of Ephesians 2:8–9?

2. Read 2 Timothy 1:9. What does this verse add to your understanding of Ephesians 2:8–9?

3. Read Ephesians 2:5. What does this verse add to your understanding of verses 8–9?

Questions for Romans 5

4. Read James 1:2–5. What do these verses add to your understanding of Romans 5:1–5?

5. Read John 14:6. What does this verse add to your understanding of Romans 5:16–17?

6. Read Titus 3:4–7. What do these verses add to your understanding of Romans 5:20–21?

Soul Care

_____ Answer the following questions as you reflect on this week's passages.

7. What is a good work that you feel that God is asking you to do? Write it down and take action on it this week.

8. In what ways have you experienced or do you experience God's peace? If you don't, why do you think that is?

IV. Do!

_____ Take five minutes and pray for someone you know who could benefit from this message of freedom. Ask God to bring to mind specific things you can pray about for this person.

_____ Tell a friend what you learned or share the key scripture with him or her. Share a photo of your key scripture on social media and tag it with #MadeLikeMartha, or visit www.katiemreid.com /martha-resources to access free images.

_____ Well done! You completed lesson 5! Now celebrate completing this study in a way that is fun for you.

Group Gathering

Instructions for Leaders

Pray: Pray that God would enrich your time of discussion and activity during this final week. Pray for each woman by name and ask God to solidify the good news of grace and the Father's love for her.

Prep: Select an activity, make arrangements for it, and gather the necessary supplies. Communicate any information that your group needs to know.

Activity: Embrace your wiring as a doer and serve somewhere (or someone) in your community with your group. Some ideas: help with a meal at a local homeless shelter, help an elderly friend with yard work, complete a work project at church, or assemble a care package for a local military family. The sky's the limit!

Key Points

- Serve from a place of peace and strength, knowing how loved you already are.
- You have been freed to help free others.

Group Discussion

1. What is one of your favorite ways to serve God?

2. Share the key scripture (Ephesians 2:8–10) from memory if you'd like and/or share an image if you designed one (no guilt here, only grace!).

3. Of all the key scriptures you have learned during this study, which one is your favorite and why?

4. If you're comfortable, share about a good work that you feel that God is leading you to do. Maybe even ask for accountability (or help) from the group to get it done.

5. Share with the group something that stood out to you from chapter 9 or 10 of the book.

Acknowledgments

Adam: You are the man of my dreams (and my days). It is a delight to be your wife. Thank you for all the ways you've encouraged me throughout this writing-a-book thing. You put up with more than you bargained for, yet you remain faithful, steady, and supportive. I appreciate and love you more than I can adequately express.

Kiddos: You brought me chocolate. You threw fits. You cheered like crazy and reassured me at just the right times. Thank you for sharing Mom even when it's hard. You make me smile, and you provide priceless writing material. I love you to the moon and back.

Dad and Mom: Thanks for not having cable when we were growing up so that we had room to be creative. Your support gave us the confidence to go for it, even when "it" was different from what you envisioned. Thank you for introducing me to Jesus, the arts, and travel. My life is richer because of Him, them, and you.

Rod and Linda: You've embraced new territory through this daughter-in-law who leans heavily on the right side of her brain. Your meals, timely words, and fix-it projects have meant more than you know.

Sibs (Brian, Laura, Mary): So grateful for your encouragement to keep going and for celebrating each step of a thousand. Your determination to live fully and fearlessly makes me braver. Love "yew"!

Reid sibs: You make me laugh with your antics and keep me on my toes with your banter.

Brothers-in-law and sisters-in-law: What joy to call you friends. What a privilege to call you family.

Blythe: Thank you for believing in this message and for helping shape it. You are more than an extraordinary literary agent; you are also my friend. I'm in awe of what God has done.

Susan: Editor extraordinaire! Your enthusiasm for this message made a dream become reality. Incredibly grateful for the gift of partnering with you on this project and for the way you helped it sing and shine.

Ginia, Lisa, Helen, and the entire WaterBrook team: Thank you for taking a chance on a first-time author and making it a first-class experience.

Prayer team: Deepest thanks for your sacrifice of time as you covered us, our ministry, and this book in prayer.

Writing encouragement team: Your support has been wind in my sails. Thank you for your patience, prayers, and cheers.

CMCC: Thank you for being a church that isn't afraid to give room to the Spirit and doesn't compromise the Word. Thank you for not raising an eyebrow when kids dance in worship, middle-aged women present Spoken Word, or grown men weep with conviction.

Lisa-Jo: Your captivating book gave me the inspiration to birth mine. I'm honored that you wrote the foreword. Sincerest thanks.

Kelly, Christy, Jami, Angela P., Abby M., Karina, and Angela N.: Writing can be a lonely place, but your friendship came at just the right time. Your voxes, confessions, and hilarious disclosures kept me sane on this journey.

Bobbie and the Build a Sister Up gals: We have found genuine community and I don't take it for granted. Thank you for your insights, prayers, friendship, and celebratory GIFs. You're the best "grace ninjas" around.

Kate and the Five-Minute Friday community: You were the first group of online writers with whom I felt as if I belonged. You hold a special place in my heart.

Jennifer D.: You are my longest friend. Thank you for your thoughtfulness and for walking the miles with me even when we live miles apart.

Lee: Thanks for praying for me at She Speaks when I melted into a puddle of insecurity the night before publisher meetings. Your love for Jesus is contagious. You are one of my favorite Mary friends.

Cindy: Thanks for throwing confetti, being in my corner, and staying grounded in the faith. Your example and friendship are priceless gifts.

Jami: Thank you for being one of the most generous Marthas I know. God used you to introduce this #TightlyWoundWoman to grace in a way I could understand, and I'll never be the same.

Shelly B.: Thank you for taking me under your wing and sending me out to fly. Your belief in my writing made all the difference.

Jennifer Dukes Lee, Brandi, Mandy S., Heidi, Kris R., Amy Elaine, Nicole, Niki H., Tami, Abby M., Jami, Jen W., Jen R., Kaitlyn, Carrie, Tyra, Jan, Rachel, "Denise," Christy, Dalene, Lee, Kris C., "Tina," Paula, and my family: Special thanks for allowing me to share your stories.

Mandi C. and Gretchen F.: Grateful for your input with the MLM Bible study.

MLM endorsers, influencers, and launch team: So much gratitude for y'all cheering and championing this message!

Blog subscribers / "Stop! Hammock Time" viewers: Thank you for your enthusiasm, timely words, thumbs-ups, hearts, comments, and shares along this process. Let's keep finding grace in the unraveling, together.

Jesus: Thank You for loving me before I ever grasped the good news of grace. And thank You for setting me free one August day, in a worn recliner on the orange shag, in my dusty living room. No turning back.

Notes

Chapter 1: The Big To-Do

1. Katie Reid, "Words That Lift the Limping," *(In)Courage* (blog), July 3, 2015, www.incourage.me/2015/07/words-that-lift-the-limping .html.
2. Mandy Scarr, Facebook, February 11, 2017, www.facebook.com/photo .php?fbid=10158209722385287&set=pb.536470286.-2207520000 .1491933602.&type=3&theater.

Chapter 2: The Worry-and-Worship Conflict

1. Todd Wagner, "Quote #1593," Cybersalt . . . in the Cyberworld, December 3, 2016, www.cybersalt.org/quotes/quote-1593.
2. Annie Downs (lecture, Women's Retreat, Grace Adventures, Mears, MI, October 16, 2015).
3. Amy Elaine Martinez, "Unwinding in God's Presence," *Katie M. Reid: Finding Grace in the Unraveling* (blog), May 18, 2017, www.katie mreid.com/2017/05/devotional-unwinding-amy-elaine.
4. Anna Warner, "Jesus Loves Me," 1860, public domain.
5. Nicole Homan (lecture, The Unleashed Worship Conference, Mount Pleasant, MI, March 17, 2017).

Chapter 3: These Shoulders

1. Sarah Young, *Jesus Calling: Enjoy Peace in His Presence* (Nashville: Thomas Nelson, 2004), 133.

2. Emily P. Freeman, *Grace for the Good Girl: Letting Go of the Try-Hard Life* (Grand Rapids, MI: Revell, 2011), 63.

3. Adapted from Katie M. Reid, "The Peace Found in Release," *Purposeful Faith* (blog), November 5, 2015, http://purposefulfaith.com/peace -in-release.

4. Marg Mowczko, "Mary, Martha and Lazarus of Bethany," *Exploring the Biblical Theology of Christian Egalitarianism* (blog), May 15, 2013, http://newlife.id.au/martha-mary-and-lazarus-of-bethany.

5. Mowczko, "Mary," http://newlife.id.au/martha-mary-and-lazarus-of -bethany.

6. "Nan," email message to author, April 17, 2017.

7. Abby McDonald, "You're a Daughter, Not a Slave to Fear," *Purposeful Faith* (blog), April 5, 2017, http://purposefulfaith.com/you-are-a -daughter.

Chapter 4: How Much Is Required?

1. Harry D. Clarke, "Into My Heart," copyright © 1924, renewed 1952 by Hope Publishing, www.hopepublishing.com/html/main.isx?sitesec =40.2.1.0&hymnID=4122.

2. Jody R. Landers, "Let Me Break This Down for You . . . ," *Jody R Landers* (blog), http://jodyrlanders.com/2013/05/let-me-break-this -down-for-you.

3. Shannon Popkin, *Control Girl: Lessons on Surrendering Your Burden of Control from Seven Women in the Bible* (Grand Rapids, MI: Kregel, 2017), 70–71.

4. Rachel, email message to author, May 1, 2017.

5. Katie M. Reid, "Doing Less in Order to Gain More," *Purposeful Faith* (blog), April 28, 2016, http://purposefulfaith.com/less-is -gain.

6. Shellie Rushing Tomlinson, *Heart Wide Open: Trading Mundane Faith for an Exuberant Life with Jesus* (Colorado Springs, CO: Water-Brook, 2014), 87.

7. John Lynch (@johnslynch1), Twitter, October 18, 2016, 7:19 a.m., https://twitter.com/johnslynch1/status/788383931804422146.

8. Jan Greenwood, email message to author, April 15, 2017.

Chapter 5: Are You in a Swivel Chair or Comfy Recliner?

1. Andrew Farley, "Andrew Farley—The Naked Gospel (from World Changers Church International)—30.03.2014," video, 1:05:17, April 3, 2014, www.youtube.com/watch?v=GfDfNepYMfo. Farley compares the Israelites' relationship with the Law to God being in a swivel chair; I build on this idea of a swivel chair yet turn it around to describe how the Israelites related to God.

2. "Jesus plus nothing" is a tagline on Andrew Farley's website: https://andrewfarley.org/start-here.

3. Jennifer Dukes Lee, email message to author, April 12, 2017.

Chapter 6: Possessing What's Already Yours

1. Alex Tizon, "My Family's Slave," *Atlantic*, June 2017, www.theatlantic.com/magazine/archive/2017/06/lolas-story/524490.

2. Kay Arthur, *As Silver Refined: Learning to Embrace Life's Disappointments* (Colorado Springs, CO: WaterBrook, 1997), 235.

3. Kaitlyn Bouchillon, letter to author, June 2014.

4. Carrie Gaul (lecture, Bair Lake Bible Camp Women's Retreat, Jones, MI, September 2011).

5. Blue Letter Bible, s.v. *"meris,"* www.blueletterbible.org/lang/lexicon/lexicon.cfm?Strongs=G3310&t=NASB.

6. Jami Amerine, email message to author, May 20, 2017.

Chapter 7: The Middle Ground Between Striving and Slowing

1. Tyra Lane-Kingsland, "What Every Mama Needs to Know About Balance," *Inspired Life* (blog), April 3, 2017, www.inspiredtolivefully.com/what-every-mama-needs-to-know-about-balance.

2. Christine Caine, "How I Balance It All," Propel Women, www.propelwomen.org/offer.php?intid=1092.

3. Dalene Reyburn, email message to author, March 2, 2017.

4. Asheritah Ciuciu, *Full: Food, Jesus, and the Battle for Satisfaction* (Chicago: Moody, 2017), 50–51.

5. Jen Weaver, "No Such Thing as Balance," interview by Anne Watson, Declare, April 11, 2017, http://declareconference.com/jen-weaver-ep-50-no-thing-balance/?mc_cid=8d884e711d&mc_eid=8b4651d91c.

Chapter 8: Easy Does It

1. Amy Elaine Martinez, "Devotional: Unwinding in God's Presence," *Katie M. Reid: Finding Grace in the Unraveling* (blog), May 18, 2017, www.katiemreid.com/2017/05/devotional-unwinding-amy-elaine.

Chapter 9: Sit Down as You Stand Up

1. Kris Camealy (@kriscamealy), Instagram, March 22, 2017, 1:20 p.m., www.instagram.com/p/BR8tUNeglN0.

2. Dalene Reyburn, email message to author, March 2, 2017.

Chapter 10: Dear Modern Martha

1. Sarah H. Bradford, *Scenes in the Life of Harriet Tubman* (1869; repr., Salem, NH: Ayer, 1988), 19.

2. "Short Biography," Harriet Tubman Historical Society, www.harriet
-tubman.org/short-biography.

3. Christy Mobley, phone call with author, May 19, 2017.

Lesson 4 (Bible Study): A Hopeful Heart, a Peaceful Soul

1. Blue Letter Bible, s.v. *"sabbatismos,"* www.blueletterbible.org/lang
/lexicon/lexicon.cfm?Strongs=G4520&t=ESV.

About the Author

Katie M. Reid is a modern Martha who encourages others to embrace their position as daughters of God as they live out their purpose as doers for Christ. She is a trained inductive-Bible-study facilitator and holds a master's degree in secondary education. Katie holds her faith and family close while she learns to let go of her tightly wound tendencies.

In middle school, Katie recorded a lullaby for a baby-food company. Now she enjoys tuning into God's love in the middle of Michigan with her handsome hubby and five lively children. Katie broadcasts hope through her writing, speaking, and weekly videos. She is also a fan of cut-to-the-chase conversations over hot or iced tea.

Join Katie and find grace in the unraveling at www.katiemreid.com.